ABERDEEN F.C.

– THE 25 YEAR RECORD

1971-72 to 1995-96 Seasons

SEASON BY SEASON WRITE-UPS
David Powter

EDITOR
Michael Robinson

CONTENTS

British Library Cataloguing in Publication Data
A catalogue record for this book is available from the British Library
ISBN 0-947808-75-2

Copyright © 1996; SOCCER BOOK PUBLISHING LTD. (01472-696226)
72, St. Peters' Avenue, Cleethorpes, N.E. Lincolnshire, DN35 8HU, England

Printed by Redwood Books, Kennet House, Kennet Way, Trowbridge, Wilts.

ABERDEEN F.C.
– Seasons 1971-72 to 1995-96

The past 25 seasons have encompassed the most successful period in the history of Aberdeen FC. During this spell the club won a dozen major trophies, after collecting just four in the previous 57 seasons. They topped the Premier Division three times in the early 1980s, lifted the Scottish Cup on five occasions (including three in succession) and also captured the Scottish League Cup four times. In addition, on a most memorable night in Göteborg in 1983, Alex Ferguson's tenacious side defeated Real Madrid to bring the European Cup Winners' Cup to Pittodrie. More recently, the club won a two legged play-off to avoid the embarrassment of losing their top-flight status for the first time in 1994-95. Then, under Roy Aitken, they collected their first trophy in six years when lifting the 1995-96 Scottish Coca-Cola Cup.

The Pittodrie faithful suffered a huge disappointment before the 1971-72 campaign kicked off when manager Eddie Turnbull was enticed away to a similar post at Hibernian, only a few months after just failing to lead the Dons to their second Championship success. They had finished runners-up to Celtic, a heartbreaking two points adrift, after dropping three points in their last two fixtures.

Coach Jimmy Bonthrone stepped up to become manager and immediately experienced the down side of the job when his side failed to qualify for the League Cup quarter-finals, finishing only third in their preliminary section. However, it was business as normal in the League. Aberdeen surged to the top of the table with a twelve match unbeaten run before slipping up at home to Hearts at the end of November. Nevertheless they maintained their challenge until mid-January when, seven days after showing too much respect to Rangers during a goalless encounter at Pittodrie, they lost 1-0 at struggling Dunfermline. Celtic took advantage of the stumble to romp away and clinch the 1971-72 title by ten points. Aberdeen finished runners-up again. Also for the second successive season, Joe Harper was the club's leading scorer, with 33 goals – 14 more than anybody else in Scotland. The club collected its record transfer fee in March 1972, when Martin Buchan moved to Manchester United for £125,000.

After defeating Celta Vigo, Bonthrone's side were knocked out of the 1971-72 UEFA Cup by Juventus. They failed to get past first base in the same competition twelve months later when they were derailed by Borussia Monchengladbach, by an aggregate score of 9-5.

A 7-2 victory over Motherwell took the Dons to the top of the table at the end of September 1972, but two away reversals and a home defeat to Celtic pushed them down to fourth by 25th November. More disappointment followed soon afterwards as they lost narrowly to Celtic in a League Cup semi-final. A few weeks later Harper moved to Everton for £180,000.

Defeat at Hibernian meant the Dons turned the year in sixth place. Later in the term, and for the second successive year, Hibs ended Aberdeen's Scottish Cup hopes at the fifth round stage. A mini-revival in the last month of the season enabled the Dons to finish fourth and again qualify for the UEFA Cup.

Finn Harps were side-stepped in the first round, but Aberdeen's 1973-74 European aspirations were dashed by Spurs. After securing a 1-1 draw at Pittodrie, the Londoners finished the job by winning 4-1 at White Hart Lane. The Dons were defeated by Celtic in the League Cup quarter-final, while they made an early exit in the Scottish Cup at the hands of Dundee.

After starting with two successive 0-0's in the League, they remained in second gear all 1973-74 campaign, never climbing higher than third and eventually finishing out of the European places in fourth spot. Goals were hard to come by: only 46 were netted in League games – 13 by Drew Jarvie, who was the club's top scorer for the second successive season.

Goals were more plentiful in 1974-75, Arthur Graham top scoring with eleven out of a total of 66. However, the club's League challenge disintegrated during a disastrous seven week spell in November and December, when they went eight matches without a success, losing three times on the road and also to the eventual Champions Rangers, at Pittodrie. Bonthrone's side finished fifth and had little joy in either cup. They slid out of the League Cup at the sectional stage and crashed out of the Scottish Cup, in the fifth round, to Motherwell at Pittodrie.

After a disastrous start to the following campaign, Bonthrone resigned and was replaced by Ally MacLeod. The Dons were unbeaten in December and January, but this was their only good spell in 1975-76 and, after winning only one of their last ten fixtures, they finished seventh. Rangers crushed their Scottish Cup hopes at Ibrox, in the fourth round, while yet again they failed to reach the quarter-final stage of the League Cup.

It was a different story in 1976-77 as MacLeod led them to their first major trophy for seven seasons when goals by Jarvie and substitute Dave Robb (in extra-time) gave them a 2-1 League Cup final success over Celtic. A replay had been required to shake off Stirling Albion in the quarter-final, but Rangers had been more easily dispatched, by 5-1, in the semi-final.

Aberdeen led the table for a while around Christmas, but could not quite maintain the pace and finished third, eleven points behind Champions Celtic. Joe Harper celebrated his return to Pittodrie by finishing as the leading scorer, with 18 goals.

MacLeod was appointed manager of the Scottish national side in May 1977 and his replacement was Clyde boss and former Celtic centre-half Billy McNeill. The new man made an immediate impact and his side surged to the top of the table with an eight match unbeaten start to the campaign. Unfortunately they lost momentum during a sticky seven game spell in which they suffered four defeats. Rangers hit the front and looked set to cruise to the Championship; however, the Dons stuck to their task, finished the season with an 18 match unbeaten run and came within two points of taking the title. But McNeill's side had to settle for the runners-up berth, with Harper again top scoring (with 17).

Progression to the second round of the 1977-78 UEFA Cup seemed likely when the club returned from Belgium after holding RWD Molenbeek to a goalless draw, but it was the visitors who won the Scottish leg 2-1.

All hopes of retaining the League Cup were destroyed by Rangers in the third round first leg. The Gers won 6-0 at Ibrox, although the Dons gained a 3-1 face-saving success in the return leg. Even more positively, Aberdeen reached their first Scottish Cup final for eight seasons, beating Ayr United, St Johnstone, Morton and Partick Thistle (4-2 in the semi-final) along the way. However, McNeill's side again finished second best to Rangers in the final. Steve Ritchie scored for Aberdeen, but the Gers won 2-1 to clinch the 1977-78 treble.

McNeill moved to Celtic Park after just one season, but he left a fine legacy, having signed players of the calibre of Gordon Strachan (from Dundee) and Steve Archibald (from Clyde). The new man at the helm was former East Stirlingshire and St. Mirren boss Alex Ferguson. He arrived at Pittodrie in June 1978 and the club embarked on the most successful period in its history.

Ferguson's new side started the season brightly with an unbeaten six match run, but three successive 2-1 defeats in October punctured their challenge. Seven draws in nine matches before and after Christmas, when the weather took its toll, effectively killed off any lingering title ambitions and they finished fourth, eight points behind Celtic.

Aberdeen battled through to the semi-final of the Scottish Cup, but were edged out 2-1 by Hibernian at Hampden Park. One month earlier, in March, they went one stage further in the League Cup but lost by an identical scoreline on the same ground to Rangers. Duncan Davidson was the Dons' scorer.

After defeating Marek Stanke Dimitrov 5-3 (on aggregate), Aberdeen's 1978-79 Cup Winners' Cup hopes were destroyed by Fortuna Dusseldorf. The Germans secured a 3-0 victory on their own ground and just held on to their advantage, even though the Dons netted twice in the second half of the return leg.

Another German side, Eintracht Frankfurt, ended their European exploits in 1979-80. Ferguson's side could only draw the home leg and tumbled out of the UEFA Cup 2-1, on aggregate. There was further disappointment in both domestic cups. The Dons defeated Arbroath, Meadowbank Thistle, Rangers, Celtic and Morton for the right to play Dundee United in the final of the Bell's League Cup. The Hampden Park final remained goalless, even after extra-time; but United took the trophy by winning a Dens Park replay 3-0.

The Dons also had a good run in the Scottish Cup, before being edged out by a single goal by Rangers in the last four. Yet, no amount of cup disappointment could take the smiles of the faces off the Pittodrie faithful in 1979-80: for the first time in a quarter of a century Aberdeen FC were crowned Scottish League Champions.

Hopes of such glory seemed rather dim in mid-November, when they crashed to successive home defeats against Dundee United and Morton. Aberdeen had won only five of their first 13 fixtures, but gradually improved and lost only twice more. Nevertheless, they had to mount their challenge from sixth place in mid-March, albeit with games in hand over all the leading sides. Three successive home victories took Ferguson's side up to second, behind Celtic. The Dons were ultimately to avoid defeat in their last 15 fixtures, but for most of that period it seemed likely that Celtic would retain the Crown; however a chink of light appeared when the Celts were thumped 5-1 by struggling Dundee on 19th April. The two challengers met four days later at Celtic Park, where 48,000 saw goals by Archibald, McGhee and Strachan give the Dons a 3-1 victory. There were still four games remaining but, even though three were away, that victory in Glasgow sign-posted a downhill road to the title. Aberdeen lifted the Crown in style by winning 5-0 at Hibernian on the final Saturday of the campaign. A draw from a re-arranged fixture at Partick gave them a one point margin over runners-up Celtic in the final analysis.

Altogether the 66 goals Aberdeen scored in 1979-80 were spread around 14 different players: Archibald and Jarvie joint top scored with twelve, whilst the Scottish Player of the Year, Strachan, netted ten. Veteran Bobby Clark missed only one game between the posts and in front of him Stuart Kennedy, Doug Rougvie, Alex McLeish and Willie Miller formed a tight unit. Together they only conceded 36 goals, an average of exactly one per match.

6

Despite the transfer of Steve Archibald to Spurs for a club record £800,000, Aberdeen made a fine start to the following campaign – winning eleven of their first 14 fixtures and not losing until the trip to Morton on 6th December. Hopes of the title being retained were still bright until they hit a disastrous patch between the end of January and the end of March when they lost four times and only won once in seven matches. Four straight victories at the start of April only served to ensure second place, as Celtic had already got the title in the bag. The Dons' rhythm had been disrupted by several injuries in 1980-81, most notably to Strachan, who missed the crucial last 16 games.

Aberdeen's challenge for the European Cup lasted just two rounds. After edging past Austria Vienna, they found eventual Cup winners Liverpool too hot to handle and exited 5-0, on aggregate. There was to be no joy in the domestic cup competitions either; Dundee knocked them out in the quarter final of the Bell's Cup and Morton ended their Scottish Cup ambitions one stage earlier.

It was a different story in the Scottish Cup in 1981-82 as Motherwell, Celtic, Kilmarnock and St Mirren (after a replay) were defeated to set up a Hampden Park final with Rangers. Extra-time was required but the Dons were victorious, by 4-1, with McLeish, McGhee, Strachan and Neale Cooper finding the net.

Earlier in the season, the Dons had looked on course to reach the Scottish League Cup final when they led Dundee United 1-0 after the away leg of the semi-final. However, United pulled off a 3-0 victory, in the return, to stun Pittodrie.

Ferguson's side defeated Ipswich Town (marvellously) and Arges Pitesti in the 1981-82 UEFA Cup, before exiting gallantly to Hamburg 5-3, on aggregate in the third round. In the League, Aberdeen started poorly with a 4-1 defeat at Dundee United, followed by a 3-1 reverse at home to Celtic. However, by early October they were in second place in pursuit of Celtic. Another 3-1 home defeat by Celtic and three goalless draws in four matches in February spiked the Dons' guns; nevertheless they gave Celtic a fright by winning 15 of their last 16 fixtures to finish second, only two points behind the Glasgow side, the pillar-to-post Champions.

Celtic were also quick off the blocks the following season, and were not knocked off the top perch until 12th February, when an Eric Black hat-trick gave the Dons a 3-1 victory at Celtic Park. Aberdeen leap-frogged to the head of the table, but two successive defeats (home to St. Mirren and away to Rangers) in early April turned the tide against them. However, the Dons were one of a trio who could still have won the 1982-83 title at the start of the final round of matches. All three clubs won and it was Dundee United who clinched their first title, with Celtic and Aberdeen one point behind, in second and third, respectively.

The Dons' League chances were almost certainly impeded by their full involvement in other competitions. Dundee United again knocked them out of the League Cup (at the quarter-final stage) but Ferguson's boys went all the way in both the Cup Winners' Cup and the Scottish Cup.

Sion (11-0, on aggregate), Dinamo Tirana (surprisingly narrowly) and Lech Poznan (home and away) were defeated to set up two quarter-final meetings with Bayern Munich. The Dons defended solidly to hold the Germans 0-0 in the away leg and then followed up with a superb 3-2 victory at Pittodrie. Substitute John Hewitt hit the winner late in the game. Aberdeen thrashed Waterschei, 5-1, on the same ground in the semi-final first leg; and although the Belgians won the return 1-0, it was Ferguson's side who went on to meet Real Madrid in the final.

Conditions at the Ullevi were tricky with the pitch rain-soaked; however, Aberdeen started brightly with Black hitting the bar in the third minute and then soon afterwards pouncing to open the scoring. The Spaniards, in their eleventh European final, hit back from the penalty spot within ten minutes. A bad back pass by McLeish put Jim Leighton in trouble and the goalie was forced to foul Carlos Santillana in the box.

The game ebbed and flowed towards extra-time with Black collecting a head injury and making way for Hewitt. It was the substitute who finally won the Scots the trophy when he dived to head home Peter Weir's cross eight minutes from the end of the extended period. It was a magnificent all round performance which secured only Scotland's third European trophy. Remarkably Ferguson's side had picked up only one yellow card during their eleven games in the competition.

Ten days later the Dons retained the Scottish Cup, again in extra-time, with a header by Black deciding a dour encounter with Rangers. Hibs, Dundee, Partick Thistle and Celtic (1-0 in a Hampden Park semi-final) had been beaten en route.

Twelve months later, Aberdeen captured the Scottish Cup for the third successive season when goals by Black and McGhee proved decisive in a 2-1 victory over Celtic. Kilmarnock (after a replay), Clyde, Dundee United (after a replay) and Dundee (2-0 in a Tynecastle semi-final) were the earlier victims.

That victory over Celtic represented cup revenge, as it was the Celts who knocked the Dons out of the 1983-84 League Cup at the semi-final stage. Aberdeen also reached the last four of the Cup Winners' Cup. Akranes and

Beveren were defeated in the earlier rounds, before a tough struggle with Ujpest Dosza in the quarter-final. Ferguson's side lost the away leg 2-0, but battled back to squeeze through courtesy of a McGhee hat-trick at Pittodrie. Defeat by the most slender of margins on Porto's ground raised hopes of another European final, but these were squashed when the Portuguese side also won the Scottish leg by an identical 1-0 scoreline.

Yet, for the second successive campaign, the Dons did lift two trophies in 1983-84. A superb unbeaten run which included 14 wins in 16 games either side of Hogmanay put them on course for another Championship Crown. This was achieved by seven points from Celtic, despite collecting only three points from the last four fixtures. Just as in 1979-80, 14 different players shared the goals (78 in total), with McGhee and Strachan joint top scoring (with 13) and Hewitt netting twelve times. Skipper Willie Miller was magnificent in defence and was deservedly named Scotland's 'Player of the Year'.

For the first time in the club's history, Aberdeen retained the League title twelve months later. Strachan had moved to Old Trafford in the close season, but his absence was soon forgotten as five straight wins propelled the Dons to the top of the early 1984-85 tables. They stayed there through to the end of the campaign, losing just four fixtures: to Celtic twice (both away) and Dundee United (home and away). Frank McDougall top scored with 22; Black netted 17; and Billy Stark hit 15 out of a total of 89.

There was relatively little cup success for Aberdeen in 1984-85. Their Skol Cup run lasted just 90 minutes as they fell victims to Airdrie. The European Cup campaign lasted only a little longer, ending after a penalty shoot-out with Dynamo Berlin. There were growing hopes of another double as the Dons reached the semi-final of the Scottish top, but Dundee United proved to be difficult opponents and the Grampian side went down in a Tynecastle replay.

The following season, 1985-86, reaped more glory as Ferguson's side captured both domestic cup competitions. The Skol Cup was won without conceding a goal, with a brace by Black and one by Stark sinking Hibs in the final. Montrose, Arbroath, Dundee (after a replay) and Hibs (again 3-0, at Dens Park) were defeated en route to the final of the Scottish Cup, where Aberdeen met the other Edinburgh side, Hearts. Hewitt (twice) and Stark ensured another 3-0 triumph to give the Dons their fourth Scottish Cup success in five seasons.

Aberdeen had earlier failed to make it three consecutive titles, fading out of the picture after leading the table in mid-December. The Dons also failed in their bid to capture the European Cup. Akranes and Servette were side-stepped in the early rounds, but there was no happy return to the Ullevi, scene of the club's great triumph of 1983, as IFK Göteborg knocked them out on the away goals rule.

Alex Ferguson's stay at Pittodrie ended in November 1986 when he replaced Ron Atkinson at the Old Trafford helm. The Govan-born manager had led the Dons to nine trophies in just over eight seasons. Ferguson's replacement was the surprise choice of Ian Porterfield.

Under Ferguson, Aberdeen had exited the 1986-87 Cup Winners' Cup to Sion (4-2, on aggregate) and the Skol Cup to Celtic (in a penalty shoot-out) at the quarter-final stage. The Dons were already on the fringe of the title chase when Porterfield took over and they eventually finished fourth, eleven points behind the Champions Rangers.

Porterfield's side exited the Scottish Cup in a third round second replay at Dens Park, with Celtic again nudging them out.

A little more than 14 months later, Aberdeen lost in another Scottish Cup second replay, this time at the semi-final stage. A second half goal gave Dundee United the glory that night at Dens Park. However, the Pittodrie faithful had suffered even greater disappointment earlier in the campaign when their side reached the final of the Skol Cup, only to be beaten by Rangers on penalties. Jim Bett, Hewitt and Willie Falconer were all on target in a 3-3 draw, but the Ibrox side won the shoot-out 5-3.

After just edging past the Irish side Bohemians by a single Bett penalty at Pittodrie, Aberdeen slid out of the UEFA Cup on the away goals rule to Feyenoord.

Despite conceding only 25 goals, Porterfield's side could again only finish fourth in the League in 1987-88. A lack of fire-power (just 56 goals in total) hindered the club's challenge, with penalties accounting for seven of top scorer Bett's ten goal haul. Charlie Nicholas was purchased for a club record £500,000 in January 1988, but the writing was already on the wall for Porterfield.

The new management team for 1988-89 was the duo of Alex Smith and Jocky Scott. It was not long before the new men led their side to a Hampden final, a Skol Cup encounter with Rangers. Davie Dodds twice equalized for the Dons; but it was the Ibrox side who triumphed 3-2.

Meanwhile, despite a 16 match unbeaten start, Aberdeen trailed Rangers in the League as nine of their first 14 fixtures finished all-square. Again a lack of goal power counted against the Dons and they eventually finished in second place, six points behind Rangers. Charlie Nicholas was the top scorer, with 16 out of their total tally of 51 goals.

Dynamo Dresden ended the club's 1988-89 UEFA Cup hopes at the first hurdle, whilst Dundee United knocked them out of the Scottish Cup, in a fourth round second replay.

Twelve months later Aberdeen enjoyed double cup success. They exited to Rapid Vienna (on away goals) in the first round of the UEFA Cup, but went on to secure both domestic cups. A brace from Paul Mason (including an extra-time winner) was just enough to edge a tight Skol Cup final, 2-1, against Rangers in October. Then, the following May, the Dons fought out another tight affair with Celtic in the Scottish Cup final. The sides could not be divided during extra-time, so for the first time ever a penalty shoot-out was used to determine the winners of the Scottish Cup. Each side missed the target once, but it was the nineteenth kick before either keeper touched the ball. That crucial kick by Celtic's Anton Rogan was acrobatically saved by Theo Snelders and soon afterwards the Cup was heading north by a penalty count of 9-8!

In the League, Aberdeen were never quite able to match strides with Rangers, but had a good battle with Hearts for second place. A 3-1 victory at Celtic Park, in their final match, took the Dons up to second place, a spot they kept when Hearts failed to beat the Champions at home three days later. Both clubs finished seven points behind Rangers, but Aberdeen had the better goal difference. During 1989-90 the club paid out a record fee of £650,000 to bring PSV Eindhoven's Hans Gillhaus to Pittodrie. Nicholas was again the club's top scorer (with eleven goals) and McLeish was named the 1990 'Player of the Year' by the Scottish Football Writers' Association.

Aberdeen again finished second to Rangers in 1990-91, but it was an extremely close run affair. The Ibrox club held a good lead, but the Dons never gave up, whittled down the advantage and then hit the front with one match remaining. That final game was to be a nerve-jangler with Rangers at Ibrox. A draw would have been enough for the visitors, but unfortunately the home side took both points and the title by a 2-0 margin.

Earlier in 1990-91, the margin was just 1-0 when Rangers knocked Aberdeen out of the Skol Cup in a Hampden Park semi-final. In the Cup Winners' Cup, they side-stepped Famagusta; but were pole-axed by Legia Warsaw, again 1-0. Motherwell also needed only a single goal to end the Dons' hopes of retaining the Scottish Cup, at the first hurdle.

David Robertson departed to Rangers for a club record £970,000 in July 1991. His old club lost its way during the 1991-92 campaign. Two more 1-0 defeats, at Pittodrie, ensured early ends to their Skol Cup and Scottish Cup chances at the hands of Airdrie and Rangers, respectively. Yet another single goal home reversal put the pressure on the Dons in the UEFA Cup visit to B1903 Copenhagen. There was no way back in the second leg as the Danes extended their advantage to three goals.

Despite winning their first four fixtures, Aberdeen struggled to find consistency in the League. A dire spell of six defeats in eight matches, during November and early December, took the legs from under their challenge and a change in management took place in mid February. The man holding the club record League appearances (556 between 1973-1990), Willie Miller, stepped up from the coaching staff to take the reins. Their final position in 1991-92 was sixth.

The following campaign saw a massive improvement and yet Aberdeen ultimately finished trophy-less again, runners-up to Rangers in all three domestic competitions. Duncan Shearer netted an equalizer in the Skol Cup final at Hampden Park, but it was the Gers who took the cup in extra-time. Seven months later, at Celtic Park, there was also a 2-1 scoreline in the Scottish Cup final. Lee Richardson's second half effort halved the deficit, but Rangers held on for the treble. In between the two finals, Miller's side went on relentless pursuit of Rangers in the League, but it was to no avail – they had to settle for second spot, nine points adrift. Shearer was their top scorer, with 22 goals.

Shearer also finished as the club's top scorer (with 17), in 1993-94 when they again chased Rangers home in second place. They only lost five matches all term (three of which were to Hibs), but when it came to the crunch, drew six of their last nine to finish a tantalizing three points adrift.

Rangers also ended their Skol Cup run, at the quarter-final stage; whilst Dundee United knocked Miller's side out of the Scottish Cup in a semi-final replay. In between times, after defeating Valur 7-0 (on aggregate), the Dons found Torino too hot for them in the second round of the Cup Winners' Cup.

Aberdeen got no further than the Preliminary round in the 1994-95 UEFA Cup, sunk at home by Skonto Riga (on away goals). They had a good run in the Coca-Cola Cup, but it was ended at the penultimate hurdle by Celtic, at Ibrox, a single second half effort depriving the Dons of a place in the final.

However, as the season progressed, Miller and his men had more than those two cup defeats to mull over. They had won their opening League match, but before their next victory, ten matches later, they had plummeted into the bottom two. A six match unbeaten run, either side of Christmas, seemed to have given Miller some breathing space as his side climbed to sixth spot, but two defeats later he was sacked from the club he first joined as a player 23 years before. Roy Aitken stepped up from assistant manager to take the reins and immediately inspired his side to inflict a rare defeat on Rangers, 2-0, at Pittodrie. However, the fans were brought back to earth a few days later when their side crashed out of the Scottish Cup at Second Division Stenhousemuir.

Another six League games went by without a win and the Dons were staring down the barrel of their first ever relegation, lying plumb last with just five fixtures to fulfil. Celtic were defeated 2-0 at Pittodrie, but another three points were squandered in a 2-1 defeat at Motherwell. However, Aitken's side showed magnificent resolve to win their final trio of games. They beat Hearts 2-1 at Tynecastle with a brace by Billy Dodds and then defeated fellow strugglers Dundee United, 2-1, in a crucial fixture at Pittodrie. Aberdeen then secured another fine away-day triumph, at Falkirk, condemning their Tannadice rivals to bottom spot.

Having avoided automatic relegation, in ninth place, Aitken's side still had two tricky play-off games with First Division runners-up Dunfermline to negotiate before they were finally safe. A crowd of 21,000 packed into Pittodrie to watch a goal by Stephen Glass and a brace from Shearer give Aberdeen a 3-1 advantage in the first leg. Four days later, to great relief, the Dons were home and dry after taking the return leg by the same scoreline. Dodds, Joe Miller and Glass were the names on the scoresheet.

Aitken had achieved his first priority, to save the club from relegation, and soon succeeded with his second aim by bringing another trophy to Pittodrie. His side battled through to the final of the Coca-Cola Cup, coming from behind to beat Motherwell after extra-time in the quarter-final, then edging out Rangers, 2-1, in the semi-final. Goals by Dodds and Shearer spelt joy for Aberdeen in the final, with Dundee unable to reply.

The Dons returned to Hampden Park the following April for a Tennents Scottish Cup semi-final with Hearts, but ended up on the wrong end of a 2-1 scoreline.

With Rangers and Celtic slipping the field early on, Aberdeen could only realistically set their sights on third place in the League. A home win over Falkirk on the last day enabled them to achieve that target, on goal difference above Hearts, to complete a fine season of consolidation. Two club record transfer deals were struck in 1995-96. Paul Bernard joined from Oldham Athletic in a £1 million-plus deal and Eoin Jess moved to Coventry City for £1.75 million.

In a period of 15 months, Roy Aitken had got the club back on its feet, pushing those fears of relegation out of supporters' minds. It was now business as usual: more silverware in the trophy cabinet, a respectable position in the table and the anticipation of more exploits in Europe.

1971-72

1	Sep	4	(h)	Dundee	W 3-0	Willoughby, Robb, Harper	13,188
2		11	(a)	St. Johnstone	D 1-1	Robb	7,930
3		18	(h)	Aidrieonians	W 5-0	Harper 2, Graham, Robb 2	14,333
4		25	(a)	Rangers	W 2-0	S. Murray, Harper	41,236
5	Oct	2	(h)	Dumfermline A	W 2-0	Harper (pen), S. Murray	14,885
6		9	(a)	Kilmarnock	W 3-0	Harper, S. Murray, Forrest	8,500
7		16	(h)	Hibernian	W 2-1	Harper, Young	24,450
8		23	(a)	Morton	W 1-0	S. Murray	4,843
9		30	(h)	Partick Thistle	W 7-2	Forrest, Robb, Harper 3, Willoughby 2	19,304
10	Nov	6	(a)	Celtic	D 1-1	Opp own goal	61,385
11		13	(h)	East Fife	W 5-0	Young, Robb, Harper, Taylor, Hermiston	14,298
12		20	(a)	Motherwell	W 4 0	S. Murray 2, Forrest, Harper	5,000
13		27	(h)	Hearts	L 2-3	Harper, Robb	19,754
14	Dec	4	(a)	Ayr U	W 5-1	R. Miller, Robb, S. Murray, Harper 2	7,582
15		11	(h)	Clyde	W 4-1	Willoughby, Harper, G. Murray, M. Buchan	13,194
16		18	(h)	Dundee	W 3-0	S. Murray, Willoughby, Harper	13,707
17		25	(a)	Falkirk	W 3-0	Harper 2, R. Miller	6,885
18	Jan	1	(a)	Dundee	D 1-1	Harper (pen)	18,680
19		3	(h)	St. Johnstone	W 4-2	Harper, Graham 2, S. Murray	24,235
20		8	(a)	Aidrieonians	W 2-1	Robb, Willoughby	5,681
21		15	(h)	Rangers	D 0-0		33,608
22		22	(a)	Dunfermline A	L 0-1		7,243
23		29	(h)	Kilmarnock	W 4-2	Harper 2, Graham, S. Murray	12,981
24	Feb	12	(a)	Hibernian	D 2-2	Harper 2	21,389
25		19	(h)	Morton	W 1-0	Willoughby	14,230
26	Mar	4	(a)	Partick Thistle	L 0-2		11,340
27		11	(h)	Celtic	D 1-1	Harper	32,853
28		21	(a)	East Fife	W 1-0	Harper	4,850
29		25	(h)	Motherwell	W 4-1	Forrest, Harper 2, Robb	9,391
30	Apr	1	(a)	Hearts	L 0-1		7,189
31		8	(h)	Ayr U	W 7-0	Harper 4, R. Miller, Taylor, Young	8,240
32		15	(a)	Clyde	D 0-0		1,535
33		22	(a)	Dundee U	L 0-2		4,743
34		29	(h)	Falkirk	D 0-0		8,771

FINAL LEAGUE POSITION: 2nd in Division One

Appearances

Sub. Appearances

Goals

Clark	Boel	Hermiston	Murray S	Young	Buchan M	Forrest	Robb	Harper	Willoughby	Graham	Taylor	Geoghegan	Miller R	Murray G	McMillan	Buchan G	Marshall	Wilson	Purdie	Williamson	
1	2	3	4*	5	6	7	8	9	10	11	12										1
1	2	3	4	5	6	7	8	9		11	10										2
	2	3	4	5	6	7	8	9*	10	11	12	1									3
	2	3	4	5	6	7	8	9	10*		12	1	11								4
	2		4	5	6	7	8	9	10			1	11	3							5
1		3	4	5	6	7	8	9	10				11	2							6
1		3	4	5	6	7	8	9	10				11	2							7
1		3	4	5	6	7	8	9	10	11				2							8
1		3	4	5	6	7	8	9	10	11				2							9
1		3	4	5	6	7	8	9	10	11				2							10
1		3		5	6	7	8	9	10*	11	4		12	2							11
1		3	4		6	7	8	9	10*	11			12	2	5						12
1		3	4		6	7	8	9	10	11*			12	2	5						13
1		3	4		6	7	8	9	10				11	2	5						14
1		3*	4		6	7	8	9	10	12			11	2	5						15
1		3*	4		6	7	8	9	10	12			11	2	5						16
1		3	4		6		8	9	10	11			7	2	5						17
1		3	4		6		8	9	10	11			7	2	5						18
1		3	4		6	7*	8	9	10	11				2	5	12					19
1		3		5	6		8	9	10	11	4		7	2							20
		3	4	5	6		8	9	10	11		1	7	2							21
		3	4	5	6		8	9	10*	11	12	1	7	2							22
		3	4	5	6		8	9	10	11			7	2			1				23
		3	4	5	6		8	9	10	11			7	2			1				24
		3	4	5	6	12	8	9	10	11*			7	2			1				25
	2	3	4	5			8	9	10	11	12		7*	6			1				26
	2	3	4	5		7	8	9	10	11				6			1				27
	2	3	4	5			8	9		11	10		7				1	6			28
	2	3	4	5		7*	8	9	12	11	10						1	6			29
1	2	3	4	5			8	9	12	11*	10		7					6			30
1	2	3	4	5			8	9		11	10		7					6			31
1	2	3	4	5			8	9		11	10		7*					6	12		32
1	2	3	4	5		7	8	9	12	11*	10							6			33
1	2	3	4	5		7	8	9		11	10							6			34
22	14	33	32	26	25	21	34	34	26	27	10	5	20	23	8		7	7			
				1			3	2	5		3			1				1			
		1	10	3	1	4	10	33	7	4	2		3	1							

15

1972-73

1	Sep	2	(h)	Hibernian	W	1-0	Harper	16,947
2		9	(a)	Dundee	D	0-0		10,100
3		16	(h)	St. Johnstone	D	0-0		9,817
4		23	(a)	Dumbarton	W	2-1	Jarvie, Harper	6,854
5		30	(h)	Motherwell	W	7-2	Robb, Harper 4 (1 pen), Jarvie, S. Murray	11,351
6	Oct	7	(a)	Hearts	L	1-2	Harper	11,763
7		14	(h)	Falkirk	D	2-2	Taylor 2	14,165
8		21	(a)	Ayr U	W	3-2	Jarvie, Harper 2	7,823
9		28	(h)	Celtic	L	2-3	Varga 2	34,262
10	Nov	4	(a)	Partick Thistle	W	2-0	Harper, R. Miller	8,962
11		11	(h)	East Fife	W	4-3	Jarvie, Willoughby, opp own goal, Robb (pen)	10,651
12		18	(h)	Kilmarnock	W	3-0	Taylor, Harper, Jarvie	10,234
13		25	(a)	Dundee U	L	2-3	Varga, S. Murray	8,173
14	Dec	2	(a)	Airdrieonians	D	1-1	S. Murray	4,059
15		9	(h)	Arbroath	D	0-0		8,354
16		16	(a)	Rangers	D	0-0		26,375
17		23	(h)	Morton	W	3-0	Varga 2, Mitchell	7,031
18		30	(a)	Hibernian	L	2-3	Jarvie, R. Miller	21,279
19	Jan	1	(h)	Dundee	W	3-1	Hermiston, Varga, Jarvie	13,576
20		27	(h)	Hearts	W	3-1	Jarvie 2, Varga	13,282
21	Feb	7	(a)	Motherwell	L	0-2		4,000
22		10	(a)	Falkirk	D	0-0		4,897
23		17	(h)	Ayr U	W	1-0	Jarvie	8,538
24		20	(a)	Dumbarton	W	6-0	Purdie 2, Forrest, opp own goal, Varga, Jarvie	7,852
25	Mar	3	(a)	Celtic	L	0-2		36,245
26		7	(a)	St. Johnstone	L	0-1		4,389
27		10	(h)	Partick Thistle	D	0-0		8,994
28		24	(a)	Kilmarnock	W	2-0	Robb, Young	4,000
29		27	(a)	East Fife	W	1-0	Varga	4,594
30		31	(h)	Dundee U	D	0-0		8,831
31	Apr	7	(h)	Airdrieonians	W	5-1	Jarvie 3, Robb, S. Murray	6,500
32		14	(a)	Arbroath	D	1-1	Varga	4,757
33		21	(h)	Rangers	D	2-2	Hermiston (pen), Taylor	32,000
34		28	(a)	Morton	W	2-1	Young, Jarvie	3,000

FINAL LEAGUE POSITION: 4th in Division One

Appearances

Sub. Appearances

Goals

16

Clark	Murray G	Hermiston	Murray S	Boel	Young	Willoughby	Robb	Harper	Jarvie	Taylor	Buchan G	Geoghegan	Forrest	Graham	Miller R	Varga	Mitchell	Wilson	Smith	Williamson	Purdie	Street	Thomson	Miller W	
1	2	3	4*	5	6	7	8	9	10	11	12														1
		3	4	5	6	2	8	9	10*	11		1	7	12											2
1	4	3		5	6	2	8	9	10	11	7*			12											3
1		3	4	5	6	2	8	9	10		7			11*	12										4
1	5	3	4		6	2	8	9	10	11				7*	12										5
1	5	3	4		6	2	8	9	10				7	11*	12										6
1		3	4	5	2		8	9	10	6				12	11*	7									7
1		3	4	5	2		8	9	10	6					7	11									8
1		3	4	5*	2		8	9	10	6				12	7	11									9
1	2	3	4				8	9	10	6					11	7	5								10
1		3	4		2		8		10	6			9		11	7	5								11
1	5	3	4		2		8	9	10	6					11	7									12
1	5	3	4		2		8	9	10	6					11	7									13
1		3	4	5	2		8	9	10	6					11	7									14
1		3	4	5	2		8		10	6	12		9		11*	7									15
1		3	4	5	2				10						11	7		9	6	8					16
1		3	4	5	2				10						11	7		9	6	8					17
1		3		5	2*				10		12		4		11	7		9	6	8					18
1		3		5	2				10		12		4		11	7		9	6	8*					19
1		3	4	5	2				10				8		11	7		9	6						20
1		3	4	5	2				10				8		11	7*		9	6	12					21
1		3	4	5	2				10	11			8			7		9	6						22
1		3	4	5					10	11			8			7		9	6	2					23
1		3	4	5	12				10				9	8*		7			6	2	11				24
1		3	4	5	6				10				9	8		7				2	11				25
1		3		5	12				10	6			9	8		7			4	2	11*				26
1		3	4	5					10*	11			9	8		7			6	2		12			27
1		3	7	5	8				10				9	11					6	2			4		28
1		3	7	5	8					12			9	11			10		6	2			4*		29
1		3	7*	5	12	8							9	11			10		6	2			4		30
1		3	7	5	12	8							9	11*			10		6	2			4		31
1			7	5									9	11*	12		10		6	2		8	4		32
1		3	7	5	12								9	8			10		6*	2			4		33
1		3	6	5									9	8		7	10			2			4	12	34
33	7	33	29	6	30	22	19	13	33	18	4	1	11	19	13	26	12	9	13	12	3	1	7		
			1		4		1			4			4	4					1		1		1		
		2	4		2	1	4	11	15	4			1		2		10	1			2				

1973-74

1	Sep	1	(a)	Motherwell	D	0-0	6,083
2		8	(h)	Dundee	D	0-0	9,517
3		15	(a)	St. Johnstone	W	2-1	R. Miller, Hair	4,000
4		29	(a)	Clyde	W	3-1	Robb 2, Jarvie	2,375
5	Oct	6	(h)	Hibernian	D	1-1	Jarvie	13,954
6		13	(a)	Dumbarton	W	1-0	Jarvie	3,000
7		20	(h)	Dunfermline A	D	0-0		7,351
8		27	(h)	Dundee U	W	3-1	Graham, Robb, Jarvie	7,081
9	Nov	3	(a)	Morton	L	0-2		4,000
10		10	(a)	Falkirk	W	3-1	Robb 2, Jarvie	3,500
11		17	(h)	Hearts	W	3-1	opp own goal, W. Miller, Jarvie	11,000
12		24	(a)	East Fife	D	2-2	Hermiston (pen), Robb	2,597
13	Dec	22	(a)	Arbroath	W	3-1	Taylor 3	2,711
14		29	(h)	Motherwell	D	0-0		8,000
15	Jan	1	(a)	Dundee	D	1-1	Graham	9,451
16		5	(h)	St. Johnstone	L	0-1		6,000
17		12	(a)	Rangers	D	1-1	Purdie	16,000
18		19	(h)	Clyde	D	1-1	Jarvie	7,000
19	Feb	2	(a)	Hibernian	L	1-3	Robb	15,700
20		9	(h)	Dumbarton	W	3-0	Young, Robb, Jarvie	4,000
21		24	(a)	Dunfermline A	D	0-0		6,959
22	Mar	3	(a)	Dundee U	W	3-0	Robb, 2 Opp own goals	6,500
23		9	(h)	Morton	D	0-0		5,000
24		16	(h)	Falkirk	W	6-0	Young, Jarvie 4, Robb	5,500
25		23	(a)	Hearts	D	0-0		13,500
26		30	(h)	East Fife	W	2-0	Graham, Jarvie	5,000
27	Apr	6	(a)	Ayr U	D	0-0		5,000
28		8	(a)	Partick Thistle	L	0-2		3,500
29		13	(h)	Partick Thistle	W	2-0	Robb, J. Smith	6,000
30		17	(h)	Rangers	D	1-1	Opp own goal	18,000
31		20	(a)	Celtic	L	0-2		31,000
32		24	(h)	Ayr U	W	2-1	Thomson, McCall	3,945
33		27	(h)	Arbroath	D	2-2	McLelland, McCall	4,000
34		29	(h)	Celtic	D	0-0		14,000

FINAL LEAGUE POSITION: 4th in Division One

Appearances

Sub. Appearances

Goals

Clark	Hair	Willoughby	Thomson	Young	Miller W	Smith	Graham	Taylor	Jarvie	Miller R	Purdie	Hermiston	Craig	Robb	Mitchell	Miller J	Boel	Williamson	McCall	Henry	Street	McLelland	Pirie	Davidson	No.
1	2	3	4	5	6	7	8	9	10	11*	12														1
1	2		4	5	6	7	8	9	10	12	11*	3													2
1	2	7	4	5	6		8	9	10	11		3	12												3
1	2	7	4	5	6			9	10		11	3		8											4
1	2		4	5	6	7		9	10	11		3		8											5
1	2	7	4*	5	6		12	9	10	11		3		8											6
1	2	7*	4	5	6		11	9†	10	12		3	14	8											7
1	2		4	5	6	10	7	11	9			3		8											8
1	2	10	4	5			7	12	9	11*		3		8	6										9
1	2	7	4	5	6	10	11*		9			3		8		12									10
1	2		4	5	6	10*	11		9			3	12	8		7									11
1			4	5	6		11		9			3	10	8		7	2								12
1		12	4	5	6		11	8	9			3	10			7*	2								13
1		12	4	5	6		11	8	9			3	10			7*	2								14
1	7		4	5	6	12	11		9*		12	3	10†				2	8							15
1		12	4	5	6	10	7*	8			11	3					2		9						16
1			4*	5	6	8	7	9			11	3					2	12	10						17
1			4	5	6*	12		7	9		11	3		8			2		10						18
1				5	6	8	7	10	9		11*	3		8				2		12					19
1		12		5	6	8	11		9			2		8					10	7*		3			20
1			4	5	6	7*	11		9			2	12	8					10			3			21
1			4	5	6	7	11		9			2		8					10			3			22
1			4	5	6	7	11		9			2		8					10			3			23
1			4	5	6*	7	11	12	10			2		8								3	9		24
1	6		4	5		7*	11	12	10			2		8								3	9		25
1	6		4	5		7	11		10			2		8								3	9		26
1			4	5	6	7	11		10			2		8								3	9		27
1	8		4	5	6*	7	11		10			2								12		3	9†	14	28
1	9		4	5	6	7	11		10			2		8								3			29
1			4	5	6*	7	11		10			2		8						12		3	9		30
1	8		4	5	6	7	11		10*			2								12		3	9	14	31
1	8†		4	5*	6	7	11		10			2						12	9			3		14	32
1			4	5	6	7	11		10			2		8								3	9*	12	33
1	4			5	6	7	11		10			2		8								3	9*	12	34
34	18	8	31	34	31	23	31	14	32	5	6	33	5	21	1	4	7	2	4	6	1	15	9		
	3	1		2	1	3			2	2			4			1		2	3		1		5			
	1		1	2	1	1	3	3	13	1	1	1		11				2				1			

1974-75

1	Aug	31	(h)	Hibernian	L	2-3	Purdie, Pirie	13,000
2	Sep	7	(a)	Dundee	W	1-0	Purdie	6,400
3		14	(h)	St. Johnstone	W	3-1	Jarvie, Hair, Graham	7,000
4		21	(a)	Kilmarnock	L	0-1		5,000
5		28	(h)	Aidrieonians	W	1-0	Young	5,000
6	Oct	5	(a)	Hearts	W	4-1	Purdie, Graham, Smith, McCall	8,500
7		12	(h)	Ayr U	W	3-0	Jarvie, Purdie (pen), McCall	6,000
8		19	(a)	Dumbarton	W	3-2	McCall, Jarvie, Graham	4,000
9		26	(h)	Arbroath	W	5-1	Williamson 2, McCall 2, Purdie	7,000
10	Nov	2	(a)	Celtic	L	0-1		29,000
11		9	(h)	Partick Thistle	D	1-1	Purdie	8,000
12		16	(h)	Morton	D	3-3	McCall, Young, Graham	7,500
13		27	(a)	Dundee U	L	0-4		8,000
14		30	(a)	Motherwell	L	1-2	Graham	3,500
15	Dec	7	(h)	Rangers	L	1-2	Hair	25,000
16		14	(a)	Clyde	D	1-1	Purdie	2,050
17		21	(h)	Dunfermline Ath	D	1-1	Hair	5,000
18		28	(a)	Hibernian	W	1-0	Pirie	13,200
19	Jan	1	(h)	Dundee	W	4-0	Opp own goal, Pirie, Jarvie, Hair	12,000
20		4	(a)	St. Johnstone	D	1-1	Davidson	4,500
21		11	(h)	Kilmarnock	W	4-0	Jarvie, Young, Pirie (pen), Graham	8,500
22	Feb	1	(h)	Hearts	D	2-2	McLelland, Jarvie	11,000
23		8	(a)	Ayr U	L	0-2		5,000
24		22	(h)	Dumbarton	D	1-1	Graham	9,000
25	Mar	1	(a)	Arbroath	W	2-1	Williamson, Graham	3,100
26		4	(a)	Airdrieonians	D	2-2	Graham, Davidson	4,000
27		12	(h)	Celtic	W	3-2	Williamson 3 (1 pen)	15,500
28		15	(a)	Partick Thistle	L	0-1		5,000
29		22	(a)	Morton	W	3-0	Robb, Williamson, Graham	2,500
30		29	(h)	Dundee U	W	2-0	Williamson, Hermiston (pen)	8,000
31	Apr	12	(a)	Rangers	L	2-3	Williamson, Hermiston (pen)	40,000
32		19	(h)	Clyde	W	4-1	Hermiston (pen), Jarvie 2, W. Miller	3,300
33		23	(h)	Motherwell	D	2-2	Jarvie, Garham	8,000
34		26	(a)	Dunfermline Ath	W	3-1	Robb 3	3,500

FINAL LEAGUE POSITION: 5th in Division One

Appearances

Sub. Appearances

Goals

Clark	Hermiston	McLelland	Smith	Young	Miller W	Purdie	Hair	Thomson	Jarvie	Graham	Pirie	Williamson	Davidson	McCall	Craig	Geogheghan	Street	Henry	Cooper	Ward	Robb	Campbell	McMaster	No.
1	2	3	4	5	6	7	8	9	10*	11	12													1
1	2†	3	4	5	6	7	8	9*	12	11	10	14												2
1	2	3	4	5	6	7	8	9	12	11	10*	14												3
1		3	4	5	6	7*	8	9†	10	11	14	2	12											4
1		3	4	5	6	7*	8		10	11	9	2		12										5
1		3	4		6	7	12	5*	10	11	9†	2		14	8									6
1		3	4	5	6	7			10	11		2		9	8									7
1		3	4*	5	6	7		12	10	11		2		9	8									8
1		3	4	5	6	7			10	11		2		9	8									9
1		3	4	5	6	7			10	11		2		9	8									10
1		3	4	5	6	7			10	11		2	12	9*	8†									11
1	12	3	4*	5	6				10	11	14	2	7	9	8†									12
	12	3	4*	5	6	7			10	11		2	14	9	8	1								13
1	4	3		5	6	7	2		10	11				8	9									14
1	4	3		5	6	7	2	8	9	11							10							15
1	4*	3		5	6	7	2		10	11	12			9	8									16
1		3		5	6	7	2	4	10†	11			12	14			9	8*						17
1		3		5	6	7	2	4	12	11	9†	10	14					8*						18
1		3		5	6	7	2	4	12	11	9*	10	14					8†						19
1		3		5	6	7	2	4	12	11	9*	10	14					8†						20
1		3		5	6	7	2	4	9	11	12	10†	14					8*						21
1		3	12	5	6	7	2	4	9	11		10						8*						22
1		3	12	5	6	7†	2	4	9	11		10*	14					8						23
1		3	12	5	6	7†	2	4*	9	11		10	14					8						24
1		3	4	5	6	7*	2		9	11		10	12					8						25
1		3	4	5	6	7*	2		9	11		10	12					8†	14					26
1		3	8	5	6*	7	2	4	9	11†		10	14	12										27
1	3		8		6	7	2	4*		11		10	12	9					5					28
1	4	3	7		6		2*			11		10		9					5	8	12			29
1	4	3	7	5	6		2		9	11		10								8				30
1	4	3	7	5	6		2		9	11		10								8				31
1	4	3	7	5	6		2		9	11		10*								8	12			32
1	4	3	7	5	6		2		9	11		10								8				33
1	4	3	7	5	6		2		9	11		10*	12							8				34
33	13	33	23	31	34	27	26	16	27	34	7	27	2	10	8	1	3	11		2	6			
2	2				1	1	5				4	4	14	4			1			1	1			
3	1	1	3	1	7	4		9	11	4	9	2	6					4						

1975-76

1	Aug	30	(a)	Dundee	L	2-3	Smith, Williamson	6,000
2	Sep	6	(h)	Motherwell	D	2-2	Robb, Williamson	5,500
3		13	(h)	Dundee U	L	1-3	Scott	5,500
4		20	(a)	Hearts	D	2-2	Scott, Williamson	9,500
5		27	(h)	Ayr U	W	3-1	Williamson, Scott 2	4,500
6	Oct	4	(a)	Rangers	L	0-1		22,000
7		11	(h)	Celtic	L	1-2	Scott	17,900
8		18	(h)	St. Johnstone	W	2-0	Price 2	5,100
9		25	(a)	Hibernian	L	1-3	Robb	11,133
10	Nov	1	(h)	Dundee	W	2-0	Scott, Williamson (pen)	6,312
11		8	(a)	Motherwell	L	0-3		6,294
12		15	(a)	Dundee U	W	2-1	Williamson (pen), Scott	4,704
13		22	(h)	Hearts	D	0-0		11,390
14		29	(a)	Ayr U	L	0-1		6,000
15	Dec	6	(h)	Rangers	W	1-0	Jarvie	19,565
16		13	(a)	Celtic	W	2-0	Jarvie, Graham	24,000
17		20	(a)	St. Johnstone	D	1-1	Williamson	3,500
18		27	(h)	Hibernian	D	2-2	McMaster, Williamson	17,630
19	Jan	1	(a)	Dundee	W	3-1	Robb, Scott, Graham	10,000
20		3	(h)	Motherwell	D	0-0		16,177
21		10	(a)	Dundee U	W	5-3	Graham 2, Scott 3 (2 pens)	9,581
22		17	(a)	Hearts	D	3-3	McMaster, Scott, Pirie	10,300
23		31	(h)	Ayr U	W	2-1	Pirie, McMaster	9,920
24	Feb	7	(a)	Rangers	L	1-2	Pirie	30,000
25		21	(h)	Celtic	L	0-1		18,221
26		28	(h)	St. Johnstone	W	3-0	Pirie 2, Scott	5,920
27	Mar	13	(h)	Dundee	L	0-1		6,000
28		20	(a)	Motherwell	L	1-2	Fleming	5,908
29		27	(a)	Dundee U	L	0-1		4,875
30		31	(a)	Hibernian	L	2-3	Scott, Fleming	4,082
31	Apr	7	(h)	Hearts	L	0-3		8,500
32		10	(a)	Ayr U	D	1-1	Jarvie	5,700
33		14	(h)	Rangers	D	0-0		17,965
34		17	(a)	Celtic	D	1-1	Opp own goal	29,000
35		21	(a)	St. Johnstone	L	0-2		2,500
36		24	(h)	Hibernian	W	3-0	Jarvie, Smith, Robb	10,985

FINAL LEAGUE POSITION: 7th in Premier Division

Appearances

Sub. Appearances

Goals

Clark	Hair	McLelland	Scott	Young	Miller	Smith	Robb	McMaster	Williamson	Graham	Jarvie	Pirie	Thomson	Geoghegan	Ward	Hather	Cooper	Henry	Rougvie	McCall	Garner	Fleming	Campbell	Street	Docherty	Gibson	
1	2	3	4	5	6	7	8	9*	10	11	12																1
1	2*	3	4	5	6	7	8	9†	10	11		12	14														2
	2	3	4	5*	6	7	8		10	11	9	12		1													3
	2	3	4		6	7*	8		10	11	9		12	1	5												4
	2	3	4		6	7*	8		10	11	9			1	5	12											5
	2	3	4			6		10*	11	9			7	1	5		12										6
1	4	3*	7		6		8		12	11	9		2		5				10								7
1	2		7		6	4	8		3	11	10*	9	5							12							8
1	2		7		6	4	9	12	3	11	10*	9	5														9
1	2		7		6	4	8	12	3	11	10	9*	5														10
1	2		7		6	4	8		3	11	9		5					10									11
1	2		7		6	4	8	10*	3	11	9		5	12													12
	2		7		6	4	8*	10	3	11	9	12	5	1													13
	2	14	7		6	4	8	10†	3	11	9*		5	1					12								14
		3	7		6	4	8	10	2	11	9		5	1													15
	12	3	7†		6	4*	8	10	2	11	9	14	5	1													16
	12	3	7*		6	4	8	10†	2	11	9	14	5	1													17
		3	7		6	4	8	10	2	11	9		5	1													18
		3	7		6	4	8	10	2	11	9		5	1													19
	12	3	7		6	4*	8†	10	2	11	9	14	5	1													20
	12	3	7		6	4†	8*	10	2	11	9	14	5	1													21
	12	3	7		6	4	8	10*	2	11	9†	14		1						5							22
		3			6	4	8	10	2	11	9	7	5	1													23
		3	7		6	4	8	10	2*	11	9†	12	5	1									14				24
1	2	3			6	4	12	10	8	11	9*	7									5						25
1	2	3	12		6	4		7*	8		9†									5	10	11	14				26
1		3	8		6			2	7	12	9*		5								10	11		4			27
1		3	7		6	4		8	11		10*		5								9				12		28
1		3	9		6	4	8	7	2	11*			5								10				12		29
1	7	3	9		6	4		2	11	8			5								10						30
1	10*	3	7		6	4	12	2	11	9			5								8						31
1	8	3	14		6	4*	7	2	11†	9			5							12	10						32
1	2	3			6	11	7		8		9		4							5	10						33
1	2	3			6	11	7		8		9		4							5	10						34
1	2	3	12		6	11	7	14	8		9†						4*			5	10						35
1	2	3	12		6	4	7		8		9								11	5	10*						36
20	24	29	28	3	36	33	30	18	35	31	30	8	26	16	4	1	1	1	1	7	11	2		1			
5	1	4			2	3	1		2	10	2		1	1	1		1	1	1	1	1		1		2		
		14			2	4	3	8	4	4	7										2						

1976-77

1	Sep	4	(h)	Hearts	D	2-2	Fleming, Robb	11,727
2		11	(a)	Ayr U	W	5-0	Fleming, Sullivan 2, Harper 2	4,800
3		18	(h)	Kilmarnock	W	2-0	Jarvie, Gibson	8,712
4		25	(a)	Hibernian	D	0-0		9,278
5	Oct	2	(a)	Partick Thistle	D	2-2	Harper, Fleming	5,000
6		16	(a)	Rangers	L	0-1		22,000
7		23	(h)	Celtic	W	2-1	Harper 2 (1 pen)	19,370
8		30	(h)	Dundee U	W	3-2	Jarvie, Harper, Williamson	18,577
9	Nov	2	(h)	Motherwell	W	3-1	Jarvie, Sullivan, Harper	15,207
10		10	(a)	Hearts	L	1-2	Harper	10,500
11		20	(a)	Kilmarnock	W	2-1	Scott, Kennedy	5,000
12		24	(h)	Ayr U	W	1-0	Harper (pen)	10,581
13		27	(h)	Hibernian	W	1-0	Harper	14,788
14	Dec	26	(a)	Celtic	D	2-2	Jarvie 2	47,000
15	Jan	3	(h)	Hearts	W	4-1	Harper 3, Jarvie	18,761
16		8	(a)	Ayr U	D	0-0		5,600
17		12	(h)	Partick Thistle	D	1-1	Harper	9,898
18		19	(h)	Rangers	D	3-3	Jarvie, Scott, Smith	21,591
19		22	(a)	Hibernian	D	0-0		11,480
20	Feb	5	(a)	Partick Thistle	L	1-2	Jarvie	9,000
21		7	(h)	Kilmarnock	W	2-0	McLelland, Graham	7,650
22		19	(a)	Rangers	L	0-1		17,000
23	Mar	5	(h)	Celtic	W	2-0	Graham, Harper	21,656
24		12	(h)	Dundee U	L	0-1		12,620
25		16	(a)	Dundee U	L	2-3	Smith, Harper	7,176
26		19	(a)	Hearts	D	1-1	Fleming	8,000
27		23	(h)	Motherwell	W	2-1	Davidson, Graham	7,489
28		26	(h)	Ayr U	L	0-2		6,057
29	Apr	2	(a)	Kilmarnock	W	2-1	Graham, Davidson	5,000
30		5	(a)	Motherwell	D	1-1	Harper	4,523
31		9	(h)	Hibernian	D	0-0		7,910
32		13	(a)	Dundee U	W	3-2	Scott, Rougvie, Smith	4,500
33		16	(h)	Partick Thistle	L	0-2		5,836
34		20	(a)	Celtic	L	1-4	Jarvie	27,000
35		23	(a)	Motherwell	W	3-1	Davidson 2, Graham	4,209
36		30	(h)	Rangers	W	2-1	Harper (pen), Davidson	13,484

FINAL LEAGUE POSITION: 3rd in Premier Division

Appearances

Sub. Appearances

Goals

Clark	Hair	McLelland	Smith	Garner	Miller	Sullivan	Williamson	Harper	Fleming	Graham	Robb	Kennedy	Campbell	Jarvie	Gibson	Thomson	Scott	Rougvie	Shirra	Davidson	McMaster	MacLean	Reilly	
1	2	3	4	5	6	7*	8	9	10	11	12													1
1		3	4	5	6	7		9	8		10	2	11											2
1		3	4	5	6	7	2	9	8*	11	10†			12	14									3
1		3	4*	5	6	7		9	8	11	10					2	12							4
1		3	4	5	6	7		9	8*	11	10					2	12							5
1		3	4	5	6	7		10	11	8		2	14			9*			12					6
1			4	5	6	7*	3	9		11		2		12				8	10					7
1				5	6	7	3	9		11		2		10				8	4					8
			4	5	6	7	3	9		11		2		10				8			1			9
1			4	5	6	7*	3	9		11	12	2		10†				8	14					10
1			4	5	6	7*	3	9		11		2		10				8	12					11
1			4	5	6	12	3*	9		11		2		10				8	7					12
1		3	4*	5	6	7		9		11		2		10		12		8						13
1		3	4	5	6	7		9		11		2		10				8						14
1		3	4	5	6	7		9		11*	12	2		10				8						15
1		3	4	5	6	7		9		11		2		10				8						16
1			4*	5	6	7	3	9		11	14	2		10				8†	12					17
1		3	4	5	6	7		9		11		2		10				8						18
1		3	4*	5	6	7†		9		11	14	2		10				8	12					19
1		3	4*	5	6	7		9		11	12	2		10				8						20
1		3	4	5	6	7*		9		11	14	2		10		12		8†						21
1		3	4	5	6	7		9		11		2		10†		12		8*	14					22
1		3	4	5	6	12		9	8†	11		2						14	10	7*				23
1		3	4	5	6	7*		9		11		2				14	12	10†	8					24
1		3	4	5	6			9	8	11		2	7*					10†	14	12				25
1		3	4	5	6			9	8	11		2	7*					10	12					26
1		3	4	5	6	12		9	8†	11		2	7*					10	14					27
1		3*	4	5	6	7†		9		11		2		12		14		10	8					28
			4	5	6			9	12	11		2				14		3	8	10†	1		7*	29
		3	4	5	6	7		9	12	11		2				10*		8			1			30
			4	5	6	7*		9	8†	11	10	2				12			3	14	1			31
			4	5	6	7		9		11		2						8	10	3	1			32
			4	5	6	7*		9	12	11		2						8	10†	3	1	14		33
		3	4*	5	6	7		9		11		2		10				12		8	1			34
		3	4	5	6			9	12	11		2		10*				7	8		1			35
		3	4	5	6	12		7	9†	11		2		10				14	8*		1			36
27	1	25	35	36	36	28	9	34	13	35	6	32	4	18	3	13	2	20	8	1	9	1		
						4			4		7		1	2	1	4	6	4	6	5	1			
		1	3			3	1	18	4	5	1	1		9	1		3	1		5				

1977-78

1	Aug	13	(h)	Rangers	W	3-1	Jarvie 2, Harper	21,500
2		20	(a)	Clydebank	W	3-1	Garner, Harper, Davidson	7,000
3		27	(h)	Dundee U	D	0-0		16,100
4	Sep	10	(a)	Ayr U	W	1-0	Harper	4,700
5		17	(h)	Celtic	W	2-1	Fleming 2	25,800
6		24	(h)	Partick Thistle	W	2-1	Harper 2 (1 pen)	11,900
7	Oct	1	(a)	Motherwell	D	1-1	McMaster	6,466
8		8	(a)	St. Mirren	W	4-0	Jarvie 3, Fleming	13,000
9		15	(h)	Hibernian	L	1-2	Jarvie	11,900
10		22	(a)	Rangers	L	1-3	Harper (pen)	37,000
11		29	(h)	Clydebank	D	1-1	Harper	9,400
12	Nov	5	(a)	Dundee U	W	1-0	Fleming	10,000
13		12	(h)	Ayr U	D	0-0		9,350
14		19	(a)	Celtic	L	2-3	Jarvie, Harper (pen)	27,000
15		26	(a)	Partick Thistle	L	0-1		12,800
16	Dec	3	(h)	Motherwell	W	4-1	Robb 3, Strachan	9,500
17		10	(h)	St. Mirren	W	3-1	Robb, Gibson 2	9,000
18		17	(a)	Hibernian	L	0-2		6,600
19		24	(h)	Rangers	W	4-0	Gibson, Robb, Harper, Jarvie	21,000
20		31	(a)	Clydebank	W	1-0	McMaster	2,800
21	Jan	2	(h)	Dundee U	W	1-0	Fleming	23,300
22		7	(a)	Ayr U	D	1-1	McMaster	6,000
23		14	(h)	Celtic	W	2-1	Sullivan 2	24,600
24	Feb	4	(a)	Motherwell	D	0-0		8,845
25		25	(h)	Hibernian	W	3-0	Opp own goal, Davidson, Miller	11,200
26	Mar	4	(a)	Rangers	W	3-0	Archibald 2, Harper	34,500
27		18	(a)	Dundee U	D	0-0		9,600
28		21	(h)	Clydebank	W	2-0	Davidson, Archibald	9,600
29		25	(h)	Ayr U	W	4-1	Davidson, Archibald, Jarvie 2	11,000
30		29	(a)	St. Mirren	W	2-1	Davidson, Archibald	9,300
31	Apr	1	(a)	Celtic	D	2-2	Davidson, Sullivan	24,000
32		4	(h)	Partick Thistle	W	2-1	Harper 2	16,000
33		8	(a)	Partick Thistle	W	2-0	Harper, McMaster	9,000
34		15	(h)	Motherwell	W	5-0	Jarvie 2, Harper (pen), Davidson 2	16,280
35		22	(h)	St. Mirren	W	4-2	Harper 3, Miller	17,250
36		29	(a)	Hibernian	D	1-1	Scanlon	11,250

FINAL LEAGUE POSITION: 2nd in Premier Division

Appearances

Sub. Appearances

Goals

26

Clark	Kennedy	McLelland	Smith	Garner	Miller	Jarvie	Shirra	Harper	Fleming	McMaster	Davidson	Sullivan	Robb	Scott	Strachan	Campbell	Grant	Gibson	Glennie	Cooper	Rougvie	McLeish	Archibald	Watson	Ritchie	Scanlon	
1	2	3	4*	5	6	7	8	9	10	11	12																1
1	2	3		5	6	8	4	9	10	11*	12	7															2
1	2	3		5	6	8	4	9	10	11	12	7*															3
1	2	3		5	6	7	4	9	10	11			8														4
1	2	3		5	6	8	4	9	10	11		7															5
1	2	3		5	6	8	4	9	10	11		7															6
1	2	3		5	6	8		9	10	11		7	12	4*													7
1	2	3	4	5	6	8		9	10	11		7															8
1	2	3	4	5	6	8†		9	10	11	12	7*		14													9
1	2	3	4	5	6	7	8	9	10	11*		12															10
1	2	3	4	5	6	7	8*	9	10	11	12																11
1	2	3	4	5	6	8*		9	10			7	11	12													12
1	2	3	4*	5	6	8		9	10			12	7	11													13
1	2	3		5	6	7		9	10*			12	4	8	11												14
1	2	3		5	6	7		9	10*				4	8	11	12											15
1	2	3		5	6	8		9*			12	7			11	4							10				16
1	2			5	6	8		9			12	7			11	4*						3	10				17
1	2			5	6	8		9			12	7	14		11†					10*		3	4				18
1	2	3		5	6	8		9	4			7			11								10				19
1	2*	3		5	6	8		9	14	4	12	7			11								10†				20
1		3			6	8		9			12	7	4		11						2		10*	5			21
1		3		5	6	11		9			12	7†			4*						2		10	8	14		22
1	2	3		5	6	10			4		8	7			11								9				23
1	2	3		5	6	10		9	4	11					8								7				24
1	2	3		5	6			9	4	11		7			10								8				25
1	2	3		5	6	10		9	4	11		7											8				26
1	2	3		5	6	10		9*	4	11		7	12										8				27
1	2			5	6	10			4	11		7	12		8							3	9*				28
1	2			5	6	10		9	4	11		7*	12									3	8				29
1	2			5	6	10		9	4	11		7										3	8				30
1	2			5	6	10		9	4	11		7										3	8				31
1	2			5	6	10		9	4	11		7	12									3	8*				32
1	2			5	6	10		9	4	11		7										3	8				33
1	2			5	6	10		9	8	4	11	7										3					34
1	2			5	6	10		9	8	4	11	7										3					35
1	2			5	6	10		9	8*	4	11	7										3			12		36
36	34	25	7	35	36	35	8	31	20	30	17	25	13		10	9	3	1	1	1		10	9				
									5		2	7	4	1	2					1	2			1	1		
				1	2	12		17	5	4	8	3			5	1						3	5			1	

1978-79

#	Month	Date		Opponent	Result		Scorers	Attendance
1	Aug	12	(a)	Hearts	W	4-1	Davidson, Harper, Archibald 2	11,500
2		19	(h)	Morton	W	3-1	Harper 3	14,500
3		26	(a)	Dundee U	D	1-1	Harper	10,000
4	Sep	9	(h)	Motherwell	W	4-0	Harper 2 (1 pen), Archibald 2	12,200
5		16	(a)	Rangers	D	1-1	Sullivan	27,000
6		23	(a)	Hibernian	L	1-2	Jarvie	11,200
7		30	(h)	Partick Thistle	D	1-1	Archibald	11,100
8	Oct	7	(h)	Celtic	W	4-1	Archibald 2, Harper (pen), Jarvie	24,000
9		14	(a)	St. Mirren	L	1-2	Harper	11,000
10		21	(h)	Hearts	L	1-2	Harper (pen)	12,750
11		28	(a)	Morton	L	1-2	Jarvie	6,500
12	Nov	4	(h)	Dundee U	W	1-0	Harper (pen)	13,850
13		11	(a)	Motherwell	D	1-1	Scanlon	5,450
14		18	(h)	Rangers	D	0-0		24,000
15		25	(h)	Hibernian	W	4-1	Fleming, Sullivan, Harper 2	13,250
16	Dec	9	(a)	Celtic	D	0-0		24,000
17		16	(h)	St. Mirren	D	1-1	McMaster	11,700
18		23	(a)	Hearts	D	0-0		9,500
19		30	(h)	Morton	L	1-2	Harper	8,700
20	Jan	20	(a)	Hibernian	D	1-1	Harper	4,100
21	Feb	24	(a)	St. Mirren	D	2-2	Archibald, Strachan	11,500
22		28	(h)	Partick Thistle	W	2-1	McMaster, Archibald	11,500
23	Mar	3	(a)	Celtic	L	0-1		26,000
24		17	(h)	Dundee U	L	0-2		10,200
25		26	(h)	Motherwell	W	8-0	Harper 2, McMaster, Sullivan, Archibald 2, Strachan, Davidson	6,300
26	Apr	4	(a)	Morton	W	1-0	Cooper	6,500
27		7	(h)	Hibernian	D	0-0		10,000
28		14	(a)	Partick Thistle	W	1-0	McGhee	6,000
29		18	(a)	Motherwell	D	1-1	McLeish	2,672
30		21	(h)	Celtic	D	1-1	Strachan	18,400
31		25	(h)	Rangers	W	2-1	Archibald, McGhee	19,000
32		28	(h)	St. Mirren	L	1-2	Archibald	10,400
33	May	2	(h)	Hearts	W	5-0	McGhee 2, Strachan, Scanlon, Sullivan	6,000
34		5	(a)	Dundee U	D	2-2	Jarvie, Strachan (pen)	7,200
35		7	(a)	Rangers	L	0-2		30,000
36		11	(a)	Partick Thistle	W	2-1	Harper, Sullivan	4,000

FINAL LEAGUE POSITION: 4th in Premier Division

Appearances

Sub. Appearances

Goals

28

Leighton	Kennedy	McLelland	McMaster	Garner	Miller	Sullivan	Archibald	Harper	Jarvie	Davidson	Scanlon	Fleming	Strachan	McLeish	Rougvie	Ritchie	Smith	Clark	Considine	Cooper	Gardiner	McGhee	Watson	Hamilton	Simpson	No.
1	2	3	4	5	6	7	8	9	10	11*	12															1
1	2	3	4	5	6	7	8		10	11*	12															2
1	2	3	4	5	6	7	8†	9	10	11*	12	14														3
1	2	3	4	5	6	7*	8	9	10	11		12														4
1	2	3	4		6	7	8*	9	10	11†	12			5	14											5
1	2	3	4		6	7*	8	9	10	14	11†			5	12											6
1	2	3	4		6		8	9	10	11*	12		7	5												7
1	2	3	4		6	11	8	9	10				7	5												8
1	2	3*	4		6	11	8	9	10		14		7†	5	12											9
1	2*	3	4†		6	7	8	9	10	11	12		14	5												10
1			4		6	7	8	9	10	11†	12			5	2			3*	14							11
		3			6	11	8	9	10†		12	4*	7	5	2	14	1									12
	2	3	4†		6	11		9	10		12	8*	7	5			1	14								13
	2	3	4		6		8	9	10		11*	12	7	5			1									14
	2	3	4*		6	10	8	9		11†	12		7	5			1	14								15
	2	3	4*		6	11	8	9	10		12		7	5			1									16
	2	3	4		6	10	8	9		11*	12		7	5			1									17
	2	3	4			10†	8*	9		11		12	7	5			1	14	6							18
	2	3	4		6	10	8	9		11*	12		7†	5			1	14								19
	2	3			6	7	8	9	10	11†	12		4*	5			1	14								20
	2		4		6	7	8	9	10*	11	12			5			1		3							21
	2	14	4			7	8	9	10*	11†	12			5	6		1		3							22
	2	3	4		6	7	8	9	10*	11†	12			5			1	14								23
	2	3	4*		6	7	8	9†	10	11	12	14		5			1									24
	2	3	4		6	7*	8	9	10	11	12			5			1									25
	2	3	14		6		9		10†		11			5	4		1				7*	8	12			26
	2	3			6		9		10		11			5†	14	4*	1				7	8	12			27
	2	12			6		9*	8	10		11			5	4		1				7		3			28
	2	5			6		9*	8	10		12			11	4		1				7		3			29
	2	5			6		9	8	10		11				4		1				7		3			30
	3	12	5		6		9*	8	10		11				4		1				7		2			31
	2	11*	5		6		9	8	10		12				4		1				7		3			32
	2	5			6		9	8	10		11				4		1				7		3			33
	2	5			6		9	8	10		11				4		1				7		3			34
	2	5			6		9*	8	10		12			11†	4	14	1				7		3			35
		5	4		6		9	8	10		11				12		1	3			7*				2	36
11	32	25	24	12	34	32	30	25	24	7	22	4	26	18	16	1	23	3	3	2	11	2	9			
		1	3				2	3	3	2	6	8	5	1	5			2			3	4			2	
		3				5	13	18	4	2	2	1	5	1				1	4							

29

1979-80

1	Aug	11	(a)	Partick Thistle	L	0-1		7,500
2		18	(h)	Hibernian	W	3-0	Davidson, McMaster 2	10,600
3		25	(a)	Dundee U	W	3-1	McGhee, Harper, Archibald	10,980
4	Sep	8	(a)	Morton	L	2-3	Archibald, McMaster	5,540
5		15	(h)	Rangers	W	3-1	McMaster, Strachan (pen), Rougvie	23,000
6		22	(h)	Celtic	L	1-2	Strachan	23,000
7		29	(a)	Dundee	W	4-0	Jarvie 2, Harper, Archibald	11,100
8	Oct	6	(a)	St. Mirren	D	2-2	Archibald, Harper	9,163
9		13	(h)	Kilmarnock	W	3-1	Scanlon, Strachan (pen), Jarvie	12,000
10		20	(h)	Partick Thistle	D	1-1	Davidson	12,000
11		27	(a)	Hibernian	D	1-1	Watson	7,000
12	Nov	3	(h)	Dundee U	L	0-3		12,500
13		10	(h)	Morton	L	1-2	McLeish	10,400
14		17	(a)	Rangers	W	1-0	Archibald	18,500
15	Dec	15	(h)	St. Mirren	W	2-0	McLeish, Hamilton	5,000
16	Jan	5	(a)	Morton	L	0-1		6,000
17		12	(h)	Rangers	W	3-2	Strachan, Archibald, Hamilton	18,600
18		19	(h)	Celtic	D	0-0		24,000
19	Feb	2	(a)	Dundee	W	3-1	Jarvie 2, Hamilton	7,000
20		9	(a)	St. Mirren	D	1-1	Strachan	7,900
21		23	(h)	Kilmarnock	L	1-2	Archibald	9,600
22	Mar	1	(h)	Partick Thistle	D	1-1	Jarvie	7,100
23		15	(h)	Dundee U	W	2-1	Jarvie, Watson	7,400
24		19	(h)	Dundee	W	3-0	Watson, Jarvie, Miller	6,100
25		22	(h)	Morton	W	1-0	Jarvie	5,500
26		29	(a)	Rangers	D	2-2	Archibald, Jarvie	52,000
27	Apr	1	(a)	Kilmarnock	W	4-0	McGhee 2, Strachan, Kennedy	5,000
28		5	(a)	Celtic	W	2-1	Jarvie, McGhee	40,000
29		7	(h)	Dundee	W	2-1	Strachan (pen), Jarvie	11,600
30		16	(h)	Hibernian	D	1-1	Watson	15,000
31		19	(a)	Kilmarnock	W	3-1	Strachan (pen), McGhee, Archibald	3,800
32		23	(a)	Celtic	W	3-1	Archibald, McGhee, Strachan	48,000
33		26	(h)	St. Mirren	W	2-0	Scanlon, Rougvie	19,000
34		29	(a)	Dundee U	D	1-1	Strachan	16,000
35	May	3	(a)	Hibernian	W	5-0	Archibald, Watson, Scanlon 2, McGhee	12,100
36		7	(a)	Partick Thistle	D	1-1	Opp. own goal	7,000

FINAL LEAGUE POSITION: 1st in Premier Division

Appearances

Sub. Appearances

Goals

Clark	Rougvie	Considine	Cooper	Garner	McLeish	McGhee	Archibald	Sullivan	McMaster	Davidson	Jarvie	Bell	Kennedy	Miller	Strachan	Harper	Scanlon	Watson	Hamilton	Hewitt	Leighton	
1	2	3	4*	5	6	7†	8	9	10	11	12	14										1
1		3		5	4	7	8		10	11*	12		2	6	9							2
1		3		5	4	7	8		10*		12	14	2	6	11	9†						3
1	3†			5	4	7*	8	14	10		12		2	6	11	9						4
1	12	3		5*	4		8		10		7†		2	6	9	14	11					5
1	12	3*		5	4		8		10		14	7†	2	6	9		11					6
1		3		5	6		8	7	10		11	4*	2		9	12						7
1		3		5*	4		8	12	10				2	6	7	9	11					8
1		3		5	4		8	12	10*		12		2	6	7	9	11†					9
1				5	4	3	8		10*		12	14	2	6	7	9	11†					10
1	3†			5	4		8		10		9*		2	6	7	12	11	14				11
1	3			5*	4		8		10		12	14	2	6	7	9†	11					12
1	3			5			8		10		4		2	6	7	12	11	9†				13
1	3			5	4	12	8		10				2	6	7	9	11*					14
1	12			5	4	14	8		3*		10		2	6	7		9†	11				15
1	6	3		5	4	12	8		10		11		2		7		9*					16
1	6	3		5	4		8		10				2		7	11*		9	12			17
1	6	3		5	4		8		10		12		2		7	11*		9				18
1	3			5	4		8		10				2	6	7	11		9				19
1				5	4	12			3		8	10*	2	6	7	11†		9	14			20
				5*	4		8				14	10	2	6	7		9	12	3	11†	1	21
1	5				4		8		3		10		2	6	7*	11	12	9				22
1	3			5	14		8		10		11	12	2	6	7	4*	9†					23
1	3			5			8		10		11		2	6	7	12	4	9*				24
1	3			5	12		8		10		9		2	6	7	11	4*					25
1	5			4	9	8			3*		10	12	2	6	7	11						26
1	3			5	9	8			10		4	11†	2	6	7	12	4*					27
1	3			5	9	8			14		10†	12	2	6	7	11	4*					28
1	3*			5	9	8			12		10		2	6	7	11	4					29
1	4			5	9*	8			3		10		2	6	7	11†	14	12				30
1	5				9*	8			3		10		2	6	7	12	11	4				31
1	3			5	9	8			10				2	6	7	11	4					32
1	3			5	9	8			10				2	6	7	11	4					33
1	3			5	9*	8			4		10†		2	6	7	11	14	12				34
1	3			5	9	8			10				2	6	7	11	4					35
1	3			5	9	8			4		7	12	2	6		11*	10					36
35	22	14	1	20	35	15	34	2	32	2	22	4	35	31	33	8	25	12	11	2	1	
	3				6		3	2	5	8	6					3	4	5	2	2		
	2			2	7	11		4	2	12			1	1	10	3	4	5	3			

31

1980-81

1	Aug	9	(a)	St. Mirren	W	1-0	Jarvie	7,067
2		16	(h)	Dundee U	D	1-1	Strachan (pen)	13,729
3		23	(a)	Airdrieonians	W	4-0	McGhee, Cowan, Jarvie, Scanlon	5,000
4	Sep	6	(h)	Morton	W	6-0	Miller, Opp own goal, Scanlon, Hewitt, Strachan, McMaster	9,485
5		13	(a)	Rangers	D	1-1	Strachan (pen)	30,000
6		20	(a)	Partick Thistle	W	1-0	McGhee	6,000
7		27	(h)	Celtic	D	2-2	McGhee, Opp own goal	23,000
8	Oct	4	(a)	Hearts	W	1-0	Rougvie	10,873
9		11	(h)	Kilmarnock	W	2-0	Scanlon, Jarvie	11,000
10		18	(h)	St. Mirren	W	3-2	McMaster, McGhee 2	11,000
11		25	(a)	Dundee U	W	3-1	Strachan, McGhee , Hewitt	10,043
12	Nov	1	(h)	Airdrieonians	W	4-1	McCall 3, McGhee	9,000
13		8	(a)	Celtic	W	2-0	McCall 2	29,000
14		15	(h)	Partick Thistle	W	2-1	Bell, Strachan (pen)	12,000
15		22	(a)	Kilmarnock	D	1-1	McLeish	3,200
16	Dec	6	(a)	Morton	L	0-1		5,000
17		13	(h)	Rangers	W	2-0	McGhee, Opp, own goal	22,500
18		20	(a)	Partick Thistle	D	1-1	McCall	4,000
19		27	(h)	Celtic	W	4-1	McLeish, Miller, McCall, Strachan (pen)	24,000
20		30	(h)	Dundee U	D	1-1	Scanlon (pen)	23,000
21	Jan	3	(a)	St. Mirren	D	1-1	Scanlon (pen)	11,100
22		10	(a)	Hearts	W	2-0	McCall, McGhee	8,000
23		31	(a)	Rangers	L	0-1		32,500
24	Feb	7	(h)	Morton	L	0-1		11,000
25		21	(a)	Aidrieonians	D	0-0		2,600
26		28	(h)	St. Mirren	L	1-2	Jarvie	9,500
27	Mar	7	(h)	Hearts	W	4-1	McCall, Hamilton, Jarvie, Angus	9,500
28		14	(a)	Kilmarnock	L	0-1		2,400
29		28	(a)	Celtic	D	1-1	Harrow	35,200
30	Apr	1	(h)	Partick Thistle	W	3-1	Simpson, McGhee, McLeish	8,000
31		4	(a)	Morton	W	3-1	McGhee, Rougvie, Simpson	4,500
32		11	(h)	Hearts	W	1-0	Rougvie	5,600
33		18	(h)	Aidrieonians	W	3-0	McGhee 2, McCall	7,000
34		22	(h)	Rangers	D	0-0		11,500
35		25	(a)	Dundee U	D	0-0		7,000
36	May	2	(h)	Kilmarnock	L	0-2		6,300

FINAL LEAGUE POSITION: 2nd in Premier Division

Appearances

Sub. Appearances

Goals

Leighton	Kennedy	McMaster	Watson	McLeish	Miller	Strachan	Hewitt	McGhee	Jarvie	Scanlon	Cowan	Bell	Considine	Rougvie	Hamilton	McCall	Garner	De Clerck	Cooper	Doran	Davidson	Angus	Simpson	Harrow	Harper	
1	2	3	4	5	6	7	8*	9	10	11	12															1
1	2	3	4*	5	6	7	14	9	10†	11	8	12														2
1	2	3	4*	5	6	7	14	9	10	11	8†		12													3
1	2	8	4*	5	6	7	14	9	10†	11		12		3												4
1	2	8	4	5	6	7	10†	9*		11			14	3	12											5
1	2	8		5	6	7	10*	9		11			4	3	12											6
1	2	8	4		6	7	11†	9		12			10	3	3*	14										7
1	2	11	12		6	7		9	10	14		4		3		8†	5*									8
	2	8	4		6	7	9†	10	11	14	12			3				1	5*							9
1	2	8	4	5	6	7		9	10	11				3												10
1	2			5	6	7	12	9	10	11	8*	4		3												11
1			4	5*	6	7		9†	10	11				3		8			12	2		14				12
1		4	5		7	14	9†		11			10	12	3		8			6	2*						13
1			4	5	6	7	12	9		11*			10	3	2	8										14
1	2		4	5	6	7	12	9	10	11†				3		14	8*									15
1	2		4	5	6	7	8*	9	10†	11				3		12						14				16
1	2		4	5	6	7		9		11				3		8						10				17
1	2				6	7		9		11†				3		8	5*					14	10	12		18
1	2	4	4		6	7		9		11			10*	3	12	8						14				19
1	2		4	5	6	7	12	9		11			10†	3		8*						14				20
1	2		4	5	6		12	9		11				3		8*						10	7			21
1	2		4	5	6			9†	14	11			12	3*		8						10	7			22
1		4*	5				9	7	11					3	2	8			6†			14	10	12		23
1		12	5				9	11	7*					3	6	2	14					10	4	8†		24
1	2	4*	5	6			9	10	11†	14				3								12	7	8		25
1	2		4	5	6	14	9†	10	11					3								12	7	8*		26
1	2		5	6		14	9	10	11			12	3*	8†								4	7			27
1	2	14	5	6			9	10	11			12	3*	8†								4	7			28
1	2	4	5	6			9	12	11	8*				3		14							7	10†		29
1	2	4	5	6		•	9		11				3*		12						8	7	10			30
1	2	4	5	6			9	12	11†				3								14	8	7	10*		31
1	2	4*		6		14	9	12	11					3					5†			8	7	10		32
1	2		5	6		11	9	12			4		3	8								10*	7			33
1	2	12	5	6		11	9		8†		4		3									10	7*	14		34
1	2		5	6		11	9	12	8		4		3									10*	7			35
1	2	4*	5	6		11	8	12					3									10†	7	14	9	36
35	31	10	26	32	33	20	9	36	16	32	3	13	8	25	5	15	2	1	4	2		15	15	7	1	
		4						12		7	2	2	4	5	3	3	4		2		4	4	1	3		
		2		3	2	6	2	13	5	5	1	1		3	1	10						1	2	1		

1981-82

1	Aug	29	(a)	Dundee U	L	1-4	McLeish	10,598
2	Sep	5	(h)	Celtic	L	1-3	Strachan (pen)	18,900
3		12	(a)	Partick Thistle	W	2-0	McCall, Cowan	3,600
4		19	(h)	Hibernian	W	1-0	Simpson	10,500
5		26	(a)	Aidrieonians	W	4-0	McLeish, Weir 2, Hewitt	2,800
6	Oct	3	(h)	Morton	W	2-0	Watson, Rougvie	11,000
7		10	(a)	Rangers	D	0-0		30,000
8		17	(a)	St. Mirren	W	2-1	Watson 2	6,870
9		24	(h)	Dundee	W	2-1	McCall, Rougvie	11,500
10		31	(h)	Dundee U	D	1-1	Black	11,000
11	Nov	7	(a)	Celtic	L	1-2	Strachan	29,500
12		14	(h)	Partick Thistle	W	2-1	Harrow, Watson	11,190
13		21	(a)	Hibernian	D	1-1	Simpson	7,000
14		28	(h)	Airdrieonians	D	0-0		8,000
15	Dec	5	(a)	Morton	L	1-2	Hewitt	4,000
16	Jan	30	(h)	Celtic	L	1-3	McMaster	20,000
17	Feb	3	(a)	Partick Thistle	D	0-0		3,500
18		6	(h)	Morton	D	0-0		7,500
19		20	(a)	Airdrieonians	W	3-0	Hewitt, McGhee 2	3,500
20		27	(h)	Dundee	D	0-0		9,000
21	Mar	10	(h)	Hibernian	W	3-1	Cooper, Strachan (pen), Jarvie	8,700
22		13	(a)	Rangers	W	3-1	Cowan, Cooper, Watson	25,000
23		17	(a)	Dundee	W	3-0	Simpson, Hewitt, Cowan	6,126
24		20	(h)	Dundee U	W	2-1	Hewitt, McLeish	12,500
25		27	(a)	Celtic	W	1-0	Kennedy	30,000
26	Apr	10	(a)	Hibernian	W	3-0	Jarvie, Strachan, McGhee	7,000
27		14	(h)	St. Mirren	W	4-1	Rougvie 2, Strachan, Simpson	12,100
28		17	(a)	Morton	L	1-2	McGhee	3,000
29		21	(h)	Rangers	W	3-1	McGhee, Rougvie, Black	15,700
30		24	(h)	Airdrieonians	W	2-0	McGhee, Black	7,500
31	May	1	(a)	Dundee	W	5-0	McLeish, Harrow, Opp own goal, Bell, McCall	6,145
32		3	(h)	Partick Thistle	W	3-1	McCall, Watson, Hewitt	7,000
33		5	(a)	Dundee U	W	2-1	Hewitt 2	6,600
34		7	(h)	St. Mirren	W	5-1	Strachan 2 (1 pen), McGhee 2, Cooper	8,500
35		12	(a)	St. Mirren	W	2-0	McLeish, Rougvie	3,900
36		15	(h)	Rangers	W	4-0	Opp own goal, Hewitt 3	16,200

FINAL LEAGUE POSITION: 2nd in Premier Division

Appearances

Sub. Appearances

Goals

Leighton	Kennedy	Rougvie	Cooper	McLeish	Miller	Strachan	Bell	McGhee	Hewitt	Weir	Watson	Jarvie	McCall	Cowan	McMaster	Simpson	Harrow	Black	Hamilton	Mitchell	Angus	
1	2	3*	4	5	6	7	8†	9	10	11	12	14										1
1	2		3	5	6	7	8*	9	11		4		10	14	12							2
1	2	3	8	5	6*	7			11		4		9	14	10†	12						3
1	2	3	4	5	6	7		9	10†	11	8*		14			12						4
1	2	3	8	5	6	7		9	10*	11	4			12								5
1	2	3	12	5*	6	7		14		11	4		9	10†		8						6
1	2	3	5		6	7		9	10†	11	4			12	8*	14						7
1	2	3		5	6	7		9	10	11	4			12	8*							8
1	2	3	5		6	7		9		11	12		10		8*	4						9
1	2	3	5		6	7		9*	10		12				4	11	8					10
1	2		3	5	6	7		9	12	11	4*				14	8		10†				11
1	2		4	5*	6	7		14		11	12				3	10	9	8†				12
1	2			5*	6	7		9		11	4		8†	12	3	10	14					13
1	2		8	5	6		7*	9		11	4				3	12	10†	14				14
1	2	12		5	6	7		9†	14	11	4				3*	10		8				15
1	2	3	5		6	7	8	9*	10	11			4			12						16
1	2	3	5		6	7	8		10	11	12		14		4*			9†				17
1	2	3	5		6	7	8*		10	11	4				12		14	9†				18
1	2	3	5		6	7		9	10	11*	12				4	8						19
1	2	12	5		6	7	4*	9		11	10†		14		3	8						20
1	2	8	5			7		9		11	12	14			4	10†		3*				21
1	2	3	8	5	6	7		9			12	14		11	4*	10						22
1	2	3		5	6*	7		9		11	4			12		10	8					23
1	2	3	8	5	6	7		9		11†	4*		14	12		10						24
1	2	3†	8	5	6	7		9	10*	11			14	12		4						25
1		3		5	6	7		9		11	8		10†		4*	12		14	2			26
1	2	12	5		6	7		9		11	4*		14	10†	3	8						27
1	2	3	4	5	6			9	10	11	8	7*	14			12						28
1	2	3	4*	5	6		10	9†		11			14	12		8		7				29
1	2	3		5	6		10†	9*		11			14	12	4	8		7				30
1	2	3		5	6		10			11	12		14		4	8†	9	7*				31
1	2	3	12	5	6		8			14	11†		4	9*				7		10		32
1	2	3	8	5	6		7*	9		11	14			12	4	10†						33
1	2	3	8	5*	6	7	12	9	11						4	10						34
1	2	3	8	5	6	7†	12	9	11				14		4*	10						35
1	2	3	4	5	6		7*	9	10	11†	12		14			8						36
36	34	28	22	32	36	30	11	29	22	25	18	3	6	3	21	24	3	10	1	1	1	
			5				2	2	3		12	7	2	10	10	5	3	3				
	1	6	3	5		7	1	8	11	2	6	2	4	3	1	4	2	3				

35

1982-83

1	Sep	4	(a)	Dundee U	L	0-2		11,700
2		11	(h)	Morton	W	4-1	Strachan (pen), Black, Simpson, Hewitt	7,500
3		18	(a)	St. Mirren	D	1-1	McGhee	4,800
4		25	(h)	Rangers	L	1-2	Strachan (pen)	20,300
5	Oct	2	(h)	Motherwell	W	2-1	Cowan, Miller	9,000
6		9	(a)	Celtic	W	3-1	Strachan (pen), Simpson, McGhee	30,000
7		16	(h)	Dundee	W	1-0	Weir	10,800
8		23	(a)	Kilmarnock	W	2-0	Black, Hewitt	3,400
9		30	(a)	Hibernian	D	1-1	Weir	6,400
10	Nov	6	(h)	Dundee U	W	5-1	Cooper, Rougvie 2, Black, Strachan	14,000
11		13	(a)	Morton	D	1-1	Simpson	2,500
12		20	(h)	St. Mirren	W	4-0	Black, Strachan (pen), McGhee, Hewitt	10,300
13		27	(a)	Rangers	W	1-0	Black	23,000
14	Dec	4	(a)	Motherwell	W	2-0	Strachan (pen), Weir	5,000
15		11	(h)	Celtic	L	1-2	McGhee	24,000
16		18	(a)	Dundee	W	2-0	McGhee 2	6,500
17		27	(h)	Kilmarnock	W	2-0	Weir, Miller	14,500
18	Jan	1	(h)	Hibernian	W	2-0	McGhee 2	14,000
19		3	(a)	Dundee U	W	3-0	Simpson, Weir, McGhee	17,850
20		8	(h)	Morton	W	2-0	Simpson, McGhee	12,600
21		15	(a)	St. Mirren	D	1-1	Black	4,500
22		22	(h)	Rangers	W	2-0	Rougvie, McGhee	21,600
23	Feb	8	(h)	Motherwell	W	5-1	McLeish, McMaster, McGhee, Black, Cooper	13,300
24		12	(a)	Celtic	W	3-1	Black 3	42,800
25		26	(h)	Dundee	W	3-1	Weir, Black, Bell	11,500
26	Mar	5	(a)	Kilmarnock	W	2-1	Watson, McGhee	2,400
27		19	(h)	Dundee U	L	1-2	Strachan (pen)	22,800
28		26	(a)	Morton	W	2-1	Watson, Black	2,800
29	Apr	2	(h)	St. Mirren	L	0-1		16,400
30		9	(a)	Rangers	L	1-2	McLeish	19,800
31		23	(h)	Celtic	W	1-0	McGhee	24,000
32		27	(a)	Motherwell	W	3-0	McGhee, Strachan, Hewitt	6,180
33		30	(a)	Dundee	W	2-0	Hewitt, Strachan	10,000
34	May	3	(a)	Hibernian	D	0-0		8,000
35		5	(h)	Kilmarnock	W	5-0	Strachan 2, McMaster, Angus 2	12,000
36		14	(h)	Hibernian	W	5-0	Opp own goal, McGhee, Strachan (pen), Cowan, Angus	. 24,000

FINAL LEAGUE POSITION: 3rd in Premier Division

Appearances

Sub. Appearances

Goals

Leighton	Kennedy	McMaster	Cooper	McLeish	Miller	Strachan	Simpson	McGhee	Bell	Black	Weir	Hewitt	Rougvie	Watson	Cowan	Gunn	McCall	Falconer	Angus	Hamilton	Mitchell	Porteous	No.
1	2	3	4	5	6	7	8	9	10*	11†	12	14											1
1	2	3	4*		6	7	10	9	12	8†	11	14	5										2
1	2	3	4	5	6	7	8*	14	9		11	10†	12										3
1	2		4	5	6	7	8	9	10	11*	12		3										4
1	2	4		5	6	7	8	9			11	10†	3*	12	14								5
1		4	2	5	6	7	8	9	10*		11		3	12									6
1		4	2	5	6	7*	8†	9	10	12	11		3	14									7
1		4	2	5	6	7*	8		10	9	11	12	3										8
		4	2	5	6	7	8*		10	9	11	14	3	12		1							9
1	2		4	5	6	7	8	9			10	11	3										10
1	2		4	5	6	7	8	9*	12	10	11		3										11
1	2		4	5	6	7	8*	9	10	11		12	3										12
1	2		4*	5	6	7	8	9	10	12	11		3										13
1	2		4	5	6	7	8		10	9*	11	12†	3	14									14
1	2		4	5	6	7	8	9	10†	14	11	12	3*										15
1	2		4	5	6	7	8	9			10	11	3										16
1	2		4	5	6	7	8	9*			10	11	3				12						17
1	2			5	6	7*	8	9	4	10†	11		3	12			14						18
1	2	14	4	5	6	7*	8	9	10	12	11		3										19
1	2	14	4*	5	6		8	9	10	7†	11		3	12									20
1	2	14		5	6	7	8†	9	10	12	11		3	4*									21
1	2	12	4*	5	6	7†	14	9	10	8	11		3										22
1	2	4	12	5	6		8	9	10	7*	11†		3	14									23
1	2		4	5	6		8	9	10	7	11		3										24
1	2	4	12	5	6		14	9	10	7	11		3*	8†									25
1	2	12	4	5	6	7	8	9		11			3*	10									26
1		4	2	5	6	7	12	9	8*	14	11†	10	3										27
1	2	3	4*	14	6	7	8	9		10	11		5†	12									28
1	2	3*	4†	5	6	7	8	9		10	11		12	14									29
1	2	12	4	5	6	7	8	9	10	14	11†		3*										30
1		4	2	5	6	7	14	9*			11†	10	3	8			12						31
1		4	2*	5	6	7	8	9†			11		3	10			12	14					32
1		4	2*	5	6	7	8	9		14	11	10†					12						33
1		3	2	5	6	7		9			11†	8	12	4	14				10*				34
1		3			6	7			12	14	11	9	5	4*					10		2	8†	35
1		3		5*	6	7		9		8†	11	2	4	14				12	10				36
35	25	19	29	33	36	32	29	31	20	22	29	9	32	9		1			3		1	1	
	6	2	1		4	1	3	9	2	7	3	10	3		2	1		2	1	2	2		
		2	2	2	2	12	5	16	1	12	6	5	3	2	2		3						

1983-84

1	Aug	20	(h)	Dundee	W	3-0	Strachan (pen), Hewitt, Opp own goal	14,500
2	Sep	3	(h)	St. Johnstone	W	5-0	Miller, Black 2, McGhee, Stark	12,400
3		10	(a)	Motherwell	D	1-1	McGhee	6,200
4		17	(a)	Rangers	W	2-0	McGhee 2	27,500
5		24	(h)	Dundee U	L	1-2	Strachan (pen)	21,100
6	Oct	1	(a)	Hearts	W	2-0	Weir 2	18,200
7		8	(h)	St. Mirren	W	5-0	Stark 2, McGhee, Falconer, Miller	13,300
8		15	(a)	Hibernian	L	1-2	Rougvie	7,000
9		22	(h)	Celtic	W	3-1	Hewitt, McLeish, Strachan (pen)	22,800
10		29	(a)	Dundee	W	3-1	Strachan (pen), Weir, Bell	7,850
11	Nov	5	(a)	St. Johnstone	W	5-0	Weir, Hewitt 3, Strachan (pen)	6,100
12		12	(h)	Rangers	W	3-0	Simpson, Hewitt, Porteous	22,800
13		19	(h)	Hearts	W	2-0	Rougvie, Simpson	19,800
14		26	(a)	Dundee U	W	2-0	Bell, Strachan	17,000
15	Dec	3	(h)	Motherwell	W	3-1	McGhee, Strachan (pen), Opp own goal	18,000
16		10	(a)	Celtic	D	0-0		25,900
17		17	(h)	Hibernian	W	2-1	McGhee, Opp own goal	14,000
18		24	(a)	St. Mirren	W	3-0	Bell, McLeish, McGhee	7,000
19		31	(h)	Dundee	W	5-2	Opp own goal, Strachan 2 (1 pen), Weir, Hewitt	18,200
20	Jan	7	(a)	Rangers	D	1-1	Hewitt	37,500
21	Feb	4	(h)	Celtic	W	1-0	Hewitt	23,000
22		11	(a)	Motherwell	W	4-0	Strachan 2, Black, Hewitt	6,000
23		25	(a)	Hibernian	W	2-0	Black, McGhee	8,500
24	Mar	3	(h)	St. Mirren	W	2-0	Strachan (pen), Hewitt	14,500
25		31	(a)	Celtic	L	0-1		19,000
26	Apr	2	(h)	Hearts	D	1-1	Porteous	17,000
27		7	(h)	Motherwell	W	2-1	McGhee, Strachan	15,500
28		18	(h)	Dundee U	W	5-1	Rougvie 2, McGhee 2, Black	19,500
29		21	(a)	St. Johnstone	W	2-0	Stark, McGhee	4,000
30		28	(a)	Dundee	W	1-0	Black	6,600
31		30	(h)	St. Johnstone	W	1-0	Hewitt	11,500
32	May	2	(a)	Hearts	W	1-0	McKimmie	14,000
33		5	(h)	Hibernian	D	2-2	Stark, Porteous	17,000
34		7	(a)	Dundee U	D	0-0		10,000
35		9	(h)	Rangers	D	0-0		16,200
36		12	(a)	St. Mirren	L	2-3	Opp own goal, Stark (pen)	3,450

FINAL LEAGUE POSITION: 1st in Premier Division

Appearances

Sub. Appearances

Goals

Leighton	Rougvie	McMaster	Cooper	McLeish	Miller	Strachan	Stark	Black	Hewitt	Weir	Bell	Simpson	McGhee	Mitchell	Cowan	Falconer	McIntyre	Angus	Porteous	McKimmie	Wright	Robertson I	
1	2	3	4	5	6	7*	8	9	10†	11	12	14											1
1	2	3	4	5	6		7	9	10*	11†	8	14	12										2
1	2	3	4	5	6		7*	8†	14	11	10		9	12									3
1	2	3	4	5	6				12	11	10	8	9		7*								4
1	2	3	4	5	6	14			12	11	10†	8	9		7*								5
1	2	3	4	5	6	7	10*			11		8	9		12								6
1		3	4	5	6	7				11		8	9		10	2							7
1	2	3	4	5	6		7		12	11		8	9		10*								8
1	3		4	5	6	7*			8	11	10	12	9			2							9
1	2			5	6	7			8	11	10	4*	9				3	12					10
1	3*			5	6	7		14	8	11	10	4	9				2	12					11
1	3	2		5	6	7			8*	11†	10	4	9				12	14					12
1	3	2		5	6	7			8*	11	10	4	9				12						13
1	3	2		5	6	7			8	11	10	4	9										14
1	3			5	6	7				11	10*	4	9		8	2		12					15
1	3	2*		5	6	7			8†	11	10	4	9			14	12						16
1	6			5			7*	14	8†	11	10	4	9		12		3		2				17
1	3			5	6	7		8*	12	11	10	4	9						2				18
1	5	3			6*	7		9	8	11†	10				12	4		14	2				19
1	3	12		5	6	7		8	14	11	10†	4*	9						2				20
1	3		4	5	6	7			10†	11	14	4*	9				12		2				21
1	3	4		5	6	7			12	10	11†	8*	9	14					2				22
1	3	12	4*	5	6				8	11†			9		7		10	14	2				23
1	3		4	5	6	7*			8	12	11						10		2				24
1	3		4	5	6	7			8*	11			9		12		10†	14	2				25
1	3		4	5	6					11*		8	9				10	7	2	12			26
1	3		4	5	6	7			8	14			9	2			11†	12	10*				27
1	3			5	6	7	12	8	14		10	4	9*		2		11†						28
1	3			5	6		7	8*	11		10	4	12	2		14		9					29
1	3	5		6	7	10	8		11		12	4*	9					2					30
1	3			5	6	7	12			10	11†	8	9	2*				14	4				31
1	3	4		5	6	7	12		10*	11		8	9						2				32
1	5	4			6		10	8†	14	11		9	2				12	7	3*				33
1	3		4	5	6	7	12		10	11					9	14	2*		8				34
1	3		4	5	6		8		12				9		11		2		7*	10			35
1	5	3	4				10	11†					14		9	8	6	7*	12	2			36
36	35	11	25	32	34	24	11	14	22	26	21	21	30	6	5	4	7	9	5	17		1	
	1	1		1	3	4	10	1	3	3	3	3			5	3	3	9	1	1			
	4		2	2	13	6	6	12	5	3	2	13			1			3	1				

1984-85

1	Aug	11	(h)	Dundee	W	3-2	Stark, Black, Hewitt	14,700
2		18	(a)	St. Mirren	W	2-0	Stark, Falconer	5,000
3		25	(a)	Dundee U	W	2-0	Black 2 (1 pen)	13,000
4	Sep	1	(h)	Hibernian	W	4-1	McKimmie, Simpson, Black, McDougall	14,500
5		8	(a)	Morton	W	3-0	Stark, Falconer, Black (pen)	5,000
6		15	(h)	Rangers	D	0-0		23,000
7		22	(a)	Dumbarton	W	2-0	W. Miller, Falconer	4,500
8		29	(h)	Hearts	W	4-0	McDougall 2, Falconer, Angus	16,000
9	Oct	6	(a)	Celtic	L	1-2	McDougall	31,400
10		13	(a)	Dundee	W	2-1	McDougall, Stark	11,000
11		20	(h)	St. Mirren	W	4-0	McDougall 2 (1 pen), Porteous, Stark	14,000
12	Nov	6	(a)	Hibernian	W	3-0	McDougall, Black, Stark	8,000
13		10	(h)	Morton	W	3-1	McDougall, W. Miller, Simpson	14,500
14		17	(a)	Rangers	W	2-1	Stark, McDougall	36,000
15		24	(h)	Dumbarton	W	1-0	McDougall	13,200
16	Dec	1	(a)	Hearts	W	2-1	Cowan, Stark	10,000
17		8	(h)	Celtic	W	4-2	Black 2, McKimmie, McDougall	23,000
18		15	(h)	Dundee	D	0-0		14,000
19		22	(h)	Dundee U	L	0-1		17,000
20		29	(a)	St. Mirren	D	2-2	McDougall 2	6,287
21	Jan	2	(a)	Dundee U	L	1-2	McQueen (pen)	21,944
22		5	(h)	Hibernian	W	2-0	Weir, McKimmie	13,700
23		12	(h)	Morton	W	5-0	Weir, Cooper, McDougall, Mitchell, Cowan	11,000
24		19	(a)	Rangers	W	5-1	McDougall 3, Black, McQueen (pen)	23,000
25	Feb	2	(a)	Dumbarton	W	2-0	Stark, Black	4,000
26		9	(h)	Hearts	D	2-2	Simpson, Weir	14,700
27		23	(a)	Celtic	L	0-2		48,824
28	Mar	2	(h)	St. Mirren	W	3-0	Stark, Black, Cowan	12,000
29		16	(a)	Dundee	W	4-0	Black, Stark 2, Simpson	9,161
30		23	(a)	Hibernian	W	5-0	Black 3, McQueen (pen), Hewitt	9,000
31		30	(h)	Dundee U	W	4-2	Hewitt 2, Stark, Cowan	15,600
32	Apr	6	(a)	Rangers	W	2-1	Cowan, Black	23,437
33		20	(h)	Dumbarton	W	4-0	McLeish, Angus, Opp own goal, Stark	12,500
34		27	(h)	Celtic	D	1-1	W. Miller	23,000
35	May	4	(a)	Hearts	W	3-0	McDougall 3	8,000
36		11	(a)	Morton	W	2-1	Stark, McDougall	1,500

FINAL LEAGUE POSITION: 1st in Premier Division

Appearances

Sub. Appearances

Goals

Leighton	Mitchell	McQueen	Bell	McLeish	Miller W	Stark	Simpson	Hewitt	Black	Falconer	Porteous	Cowan	McKimmie	McDougall	Angus	Cooper	Weir	Miller J	Gunn	McMaster	Grant	Wright	#
1	2	3	4	5	6	7*	8	9	10	11†	12	14											1
1		3	10	5	6	4	8		11	7			2	9*	12								2
1		3	10	5	6	4	8		7	11			2	9									3
1		3	10	5	6	4	8*	14	7	11†			2	9	12								4
1		3	10†	5	6	4	8	12	7	11			2	9*	14								5
1		3		5	6	4	8†	7*		11	12		2	9	14	10							6
1		3	10	5	6		8		7	14	12		2	9*	11†	4							7
1		3	7*	5	6	12	8		9†	11			2	14	10	4							8
1		3		5	6	11†	8	12	7		14		2	9	10*	4							9
1		3		5	6	11†	8		7	14	12		2	9*	10	4							10
1		3		5	6	4	8		10	12	7*		2	9	11								11
1	2	3		5	6	4	8		10		7*			9	11	12							12
1	14	3*		5	6	4†	8		7		12		2	9	10	11							13
1				5	6	4	8		7*			12	2	9	3	10	11						14
1		14		5	6	4	8		7			12	2	9	3*	10†	11						15
1	14	3		5	6	4	8	12				7	2	9*		10†	11						16
1	12	3		5	6	4*	8	14	7				2	9		10	11†						17
1		3*		5	6	4	8	11	7			12	2	9	10	14							18
1	14	3			6	4	8			7*			2	9	10†	5	11	12					19
1	10	3	8†		6	4*			7	12			2	9	14	5	11						20
1	4	3	10		6	12	8			7†		14	2*	9		5	11						21
	2	3	10†		6		8	12		7*			4	9	14	5	11		1				22
1	12	3	10		6	4*	8	7				14	2	9†		5	11						23
1	12	3	10†		6	4*	8	14	7				2	9		5	11						24
1		3		5	6	10	8		7				2	9		4	11						25
1		3	10†	5	6		8	12	7				2	9*	14	4	11						26
1		3	12	5	6		8*	14	7			9†	2		10	4	11						27
1	6	3		5		4	8		7		9	12	2		10		11*						28
1	14	3	12	5	6	4*	8	9†	7			11	2		10								29
1		3	12	5	6	4	8	9	7			11	2		10*								30
1		3*	8	5	6	4		9	7	14		11†	2		10	12							31
1		14	8	5	6	4		9	7*	12		11	2		10†	3							32
1		3	10	5	6	4	8*	9	7			12	2		11								33
1		3	10†	5	6	4	8	11		7	12		2	9*		14							34
1	2	3	10*	5		4	8	11†				7	14	6	9					12			35
		3	12	5*	6	4	8	14	7		11†		2	9	10								36
34	7	33	18	30	34	30	33	11	27	10	7	6	34	27	21	17	15		2				
	7	2	4		2		10		6	6	10		1	7	3	1	1		1				
	1	3		1	3	15	4	4	16	4	1	5	3	22	2	1	3						

1985-86

1	Aug	10	(h)	Hibernian	W 3-0	Bett, McDougall 2	15,000
2		17	(a)	Dundee U	D 1-1	McKimmie	14,500
3		24	(h)	Motherwell	D 1-1	McKimmie	14,400
4		31	(a)	Dundee	W 3-1	Simpson, Stark 2	7,600
5	Sep	7	(h)	Hearts	W 3-0	Stark, Wright, Black	12,000
6		14	(a)	Celtic	L 1-2	McDougall	39,500
7		21	(h)	St. Mirren	D 1-1	McQueen (pen)	13,000
8		28	(a)	Rangers	W 3-0	McLeish, Stark, Hewitt	37,600
9	Oct	5	(h)	Clydebank	W 3-1	Black, McDougall, McKimmie	11,500
10		12	(a)	Hibernian	D 1-1	Gray	14,000
11		19	(h)	Dundee U	W 3-2	Hewitt 2, McDougall	15,800
12		30	(a)	Hearts	L 0-1		12,500
13	Nov	2	(h)	Celtic	W 4-1	McDougall 4	22,500
14		9	(h)	Dundee	W 4-1	McLeish, McDougall, Stark 2	12,000
15		16	(a)	Motherwell	D 1-1	McDougall (pen)	5,000
16		23	(a)	St. Mirren	L 0-1		3,900
17	Dec	10	(a)	Clydebank	L 1-2	Black	2,100
18		14	(h)	Hibernian	W 4-0	Angus, Weir, J. Miller, McLeish	11,500
19		21	(a)	Dundee U	L 1-2	Stark	10,100
20	Jan	1	(a)	Dundee	D 0-0		9,100
21		4	(h)	St. Mirren	W 3-1	Black 2, Weir	11,500
22		11	(a)	Celtic	D 1-1	J. Miller	31,300
23		18	(h)	Hearts	L 0-1		21,000
24	Feb	1	(a)	Rangers	D 1-1	J. Miller	29,000
25		8	(h)	Clydebank	W 4-1	Bett (pen), Black 3	11,000
26		19	(h)	Rangers	W 1-0	Angus	19,500
27		22	(a)	Hibernian	W 1-0	Wright	9,500
28	Mar	15	(a)	St. Mirren	D 1-1	W. Miller	4,500
29		22	(h)	Dundee	D 0-0		13,000
30		29	(a)	Motherwell	W 1-0	Hewitt	4,600
31	Apr	9	(h)	Motherwell	W 3-2	Bett, McDougall, Weir	10,300
32		12	(h)	Celtic	L 0-1		22,500
33		16	(h)	Dundee U	L 0-1		8,500
34		20	(a)	Hearts	D 1-1	Weir (pen)	19,100
35		26	(h)	Rangers	D 1-1	Hewitt	17,000
36	May	3	(a)	Clydebank	W 6-0	Stark, McMaster, Weir, Hewitt, McDougall 2	5,000

FINAL LEAGUE POSITION: 4th in Premier Division

Appearances

Sub. Appearances

Goals

Leighton	McKimmie	McQueen	Stark	McLeish	Miller W	Black	Simpson	McDougall	Bett	Weir	Hewitt	Gunn	Cooper	Mitchell	McIntyre	Wright	Gray	Porteous	Falconer	Angus	Miller J	McMaster	Robertson I	Irvine	No.
1	2	3	4	5	6	7*	8	9	10	11	12														1
	2		4	5	6	7*	8	9	10	11	12	1	3												2
	2	3*	4	5	6	14	8	9†	10	11	7	1	12												3
1	2		4	5	6	7	8	9*	10	11†	14			3	12										4
1	2		4*	5	6	7	8	9†	10	11	14			3	12										5
1	2		4*	5	6	7	8	9	10	14	11†		12	3											6
1	2	3*	4	5	6	7	12	10		9†			8						11	14					7
1	2		4*	5	6	7	8	9†		11			10	3			12		14						8
1	2		4*	5	6	7†	8	9		11			10	3					14	12					9
1	2		4	5	6		8†	9		11			10	3*			14		12	7					10
1	2		4	5	6	12	8†	9		11			10	3	14	7*									11
1	2			5	6		8	9†	12	7	11		10			14	4		3*						12
1	2		4*	5	6	7	8	9	12	11†			10	3			14								13
1	2		4	5	6			9	8	11				3			7	12	10*						14
1	2		4	5	6		8	9	10	11	14			3*			7†		12						15
1	2	12	4	5	6		8	9		11	7†		10	3*					14						16
1	2		4	5		7	8	14	12				10	3*					11†	6	9				17
	2		4*	5		7	8	9	12			1	6	3					10	11					18
1	2	14	4	5	6	7		9*	12				10†	3					8	11					19
1	2	3	4	5	6	7							10				14		8*	9†	12	11			20
1		3	4	5	6	7			10	11			2						8*	12	9				21
1	2	3	14	5	6	7	8	12	10	11†			4							9*					22
1	2	3*	4	5	6	7	8	9†	10	11			12							14					23
1	2	3	4*	5	6	7	8		10	11			12							9					24
1	2		4*	5	6	7	8†	9	10				14						12	3		11			25
1	2	3*		5	6	7	8	9†	10				4				14			12		11			26
1	2		4*	5	6	7	8			14			10	12			9			3		11†			27
1	2	3*	12	5	6					10			11	4			9		14	8	7†				28
1	2		8		6				10		11†		4	12		9*			14	3	7				29
	2	3	4	5	6					10	9	1	5				12			8	7*	11			30
	2	3		5	6	7		9†	10	11		1		12			8			14	4*				31
	2	3*	4	5	6	7			10	11		1	8						14	9	12				32
	2			5	6	7*				10	11	1	3						14	8†	9	12	4		33
	2	3		5	6	12			10	11	7*	1	8†							9	4	14			34
				5	6					11	10	1	2*	3†	14	7	12			9	4	8			35
	2	3	4					9		11	8	1	6			7*		12	10†	14				5	36
26	34	15	28	34	33	23	22	22	22	17	18	10	20	18	2	3	10	2	12	17	5	2	1		
	3	3		3		3	2	4	5		3	5	3	7	3		6		6	5	2	2	2		
	3	1	8	3	1	8	1	14	3	5	6		2	1			2		3	1					

1986-87

1	Aug	9	(a)	Dundee U	L	1-2	Stark	11,000
2		13	(h)	Hibernian	W	4-0	J. Miller, Angus, Gray, Stark	13,000
3		16	(h)	Hamilton A	W	2-0	Stark 2	10,500
4		23	(a)	Celtic	D	1-1	J. Miller	46,473
5		30	(h)	Dundee	W	2-0	Hewitt, J. Miller	12,500
6	Sep	6	(a)	St. Mirren	D	1-1	Stark	4,400
7		13	(h)	Hearts	L	0-1		15,600
8		20	(a)	Clydebank	W	3-1	Hewitt 2, Weir	2,766
9		27	(a)	Rangers	L	0-2		40,155
10	Oct	4	(h)	Motherwell	D	2-2	Dodds, W. Miller	9,500
11		8	(a)	Falkirk	D	3-3	Stark, McLeish, Bett (pen)	6,000
12		11	(h)	Dundee U	W	2-0	Hewitt 2	15,000
13		18	(a)	Hibernian	D	1-1	Connor	9,000
14		25	(a)	Hamilton A	W	1-0	Bett	3,000
15	Nov	1	(a)	Dundee	W	2-0	Dodds, Porteous	8,200
16		8	(h)	St. Mirren	D	0-0		11,000
17		15	(a)	Hearts	L	1-2	Hewitt	17,108
18		19	(h)	Clydebank	W	5-0	Stark 2, Conner 2, Hewitt	7,500
19		22	(h)	Rangers	W	1-0	Dodds	23,500
20		26	(h)	Celtic	D	1-1	McLeish	23,500
21		29	(a)	Motherwell	W	1-0	Weir	4,500
22	Dec	3	(h)	Falkirk	W	1-0	Stark	10,000
23		6	(a)	Dundee U	D	0-0		10,242
24		13	(h)	Hibernian	W	1-0	Stark	11,000
25		20	(a)	Celtic	D	1-1	J. Miller	32,624
26		27	(h)	Hamilton A	D	0-0		10,500
27	Jan	1	(h)	Dundee	W	2-1	Wright, Grant	11,000
28		10	(h)	Hearts	W	2-1	Grant, W. Miller	15,000
29		24	(a)	Rangers	D	0-0		44,000
30		27	(a)	Clydebank	W	5-0	Wright 2, Connor, Dodds, Hewitt	2,700
31	Feb	7	(h)	Motherwell	W	1-0	Wright	10,000
32		21	(a)	Falkirk	W	3-0	Stark 2, McLeish	5,500
33		25	(a)	St. Mirren	L	0-1		3,553
34		28	(h)	Dundee U	L	0-1		14,000
35	Mar	7	(a)	Hibernian	D	1-1	Bett	6,000
36		14	(h)	Celtic	W	1-0	Irvine	20,000
37		21	(a)	Hamilton A	W	2-0	Bett, Porteous	3,600
38		28	(h)	St. Mirren	L	0-1		7,000
39	Apr	4	(a)	Dundee	D	1-1	Grant	4,346
40		11	(h)	Clydebank	D	1-1	Irvine	6,000
41		18	(a)	Hearts	D	1-1	Hewitt	12,539
42		25	(a)	Motherwell	W	2-0	Hewitt (pen), J. Miller	2,800
43	May	2	(h)	Rangers	D	1-1	Irvine	23,500
44		9	(h)	Falkirk	W	3-1	J. Miller, Grant, Hewitt (pen)	7,300

FINAL LEAGUE POSITION: 4th in Premier Division

Appearances

Sub. Appearances

Goals

44

Leighton	McKimmie	Mitchell	Stark	McLeish	Irvine	Gray	Simpson	Hewitt	Angus	Weir	Miller J	Falconer	McDougall	Bett	Connor	Robertson D	Gunn	Miller W	Wright	McQueen	McMaster	McIntyre	Porteous	Dodds	Robertson I	Grant	
1	2	3	4	5	6	7	8*	9†	10	11	14	12															1
1	2	3	4	5	6	7*		9	10	11	8†	12	14														2
1	2	3†	4	5	6	12		9		11	7*			8	10	14											3
	2	12	4	5	3	7*		9†		11	8	14			10		1	6									4
	2	12	4	5	3*			9		11	7†			8	10		1	6	14								5
1	2		4	5	7					9		14			10†			6	11	3	8*	12					6
1	2	3	4	5	10*	14		9		11†	7			8				6					12				7
1	2	3	4†	5				7*		11				8				6	9				12	14			8
1	2	3	4*	5				7†		11				8	10	12		6	14					9			9
1	2		4	5	12					11†				8	10	3*		6	7				14	9			10
1	2	3	4	5						14				8	10			6	12				7*	11	9†		11
1	2	3	4	5*		12		7		11				8				6						9			12
1	2	3	4		5*			10		11				7	8	6			12†			14		9			13
1	2	3	14	5						11*				8	10†	4		6	12				7	9			14
1	2	3*	12	5				9†				14		8	10	4		6					7	11			15
1	2	3	12	5						11	7†			8	10	4*		6	14					9			16
1	2	4*		5				7		11	12			8	10	3		6						9			17
1	2	4	5†					11			12	7*		8	10			6	14			3		9			18
1	2	4	5					11			7			8	10	3		6						9			19
1	2	4	5					11*			12	7†		8	10	3		6	14					9			20
1	2	4	5					7		11				8	10	3		6						9			21
1	2	4*	5					11			7	12		8	10	3		6	14					9†			22
1	2		5					11			7			8	10	3		6						9	4		23
1	2	4	5					12		11	7			8	10*	3		6						9			24
1	2	4	5					12		11*	7			8	10	3		6						9			25
1	2	4	5					12		11	7*			8	10	3		6	9								26
1	2	4*	5					11			7			8	10	3		6	9						12		27
1	2	12	5*					11†			7			8	14	3		6	10					9	4		28
1	2	5						12			7			8	11	3		6	10*					9	4		29
1	2	12	5					7						8	11	3		6*	10				14	9†	4		30
1	2	10	5					7		11				8		3		6	12					9*	4		31
1	2	4	5					11		12					8	3		6	10*					9	7		32
1	2	4	5					11			7*			8	14	3		6	12					9	10†		33
1	2	4	5					9		11				8	10	3*		6					12		7		34
1			4	5	2	12				11				8		3		6	9					12	7*		35
1			4	5	2	12				11	7			8		3		6	9*					12			36
1		4*	5	2				11			7	14		8	10	3		6	9†					12			37
1		4	5	2		12				11		9		8	10			6	7*						3		38
1				5	6	4	8	9		11					10	3								2	7		39
1	2			5	6	12	4	11				7		8	10*	3			14						9†		40
1	2			5	6	4		9	10	11				8									7*	3	12		41
1	2			5	6	4		9	10	11	7			8		3											42
1	2			5		4	7	11	10	9				8	3*			6							12		43
1	2			5		4	7	11		9				8	3			6							10		44
42	37	15	31	40	19	9	8	28	2	32	23	1		38	30	32	2	36	13	1	2	3		24	4	12	
	2	5			1	4		5		3	5	5	1		2	2			12		4	6	1			3	
		12	3	3	1			11	1	2	6			4	4			2	4					2	4	4	

45

1987-88

1	Aug	8	(a)	Dundee	D	1-1	Dodds	10,223
2		12	(h)	Morton	W	3-1	Miller J, Simpson, Dodds	8,000
3		15	(h)	Rangers	W	2-0	Dodds, Nicholas P	22,500
4		22	(a)	Motherwell	W	1-0	Dodds	4,858
5		29	(h)	Dundee U	D	1-1	Bett (pen)	16,000
6	Sep	5	(a)	Falkirk	D	2-2	Falconer, Miller J	5,328
7		12	(h)	St. Mirren	W	2-0	Miller J, Falconer	11,000
8		19	(a)	Celtic	D	2-2	Nicholas P, Miller J	38,944
9		26	(a)	Hibernian	W	2-0	Grant, Falconer	10,500
10	Oct	3	(h)	Dunfermline Ath	W	3-0	Nicholas P, Falconer, Edwards	11,313
11		7	(a)	Hearts	L	1-2	Bett (pen)	17,741
12		10	(h)	Dundee	D	0-0		12,500
13		17	(a)	Dundee U	D	0-0		11,281
14		28	(a)	St. Mirren	W	3-1	Bett 2 (1 pen), Falconer	4,707
15		31	(h)	Celtic	L	0-1		21,000
16	Nov	7	(a)	Morton	D	0-0		3,000
17		14	(h)	Hearts	D	0-0		20,000
18		17	(a)	Rangers	W	1-0	Miller W	41,371
19		21	(h)	Motherwell	W	1-0	Dodds	9,700
20		24	(h)	Hibernian	D	1-1	Edwards	9,000
21		28	(a)	Dunfermline Ath	W	3-0	Jones, Wright 2	7,500
22	Dec	5	(a)	Dundee	W	2-1	Dodds, Wright	8,799
23		9	(h)	Falkirk	W	3-1	Dodds, Bett, Wright	8,000
24		12	(h)	Morton	W	4-0	Bett 2 (2 pens), Dodds, Connor	8,000
25		16	(h)	St. Mirren	W	2-1	Bett (pen), Miller W	6,500
26		19	(a)	Celtic	D	0-0		37,721
27		26	(a)	Falkirk	W	2-0	McLeish, Hewitt	5,000
28	Jan	2	(h)	Dundee U	D	0-0		21,500
29		9	(a)	Hibernian	D	0-0		16,000
30		16	(h)	Dunfermline Ath	W	1-0	Falconer	20,000
31		23	(a)	Motherwell	L	1-2	Nicholas C	6,584
32	Feb	6	(h)	Rangers	L	1-2	Bett (pen)	22,500
33		13	(a)	Hearts	D	2-2	Bett, Jones (pen)	18,817
34		27	(h)	Dundee	W	1-0	Dodds	13,500
35	Mar	5	(a)	St. Mirren	D	0-0		4,858
36		19	(a)	Dundee U	W	2-0	Nicholas C, Jones	10,403
37		26	(h)	Falkirk	W	2-0	Falconer, Miller W	9,410
38		30	(h)	Celtic	L	0-1		22,700
39	Apr	2	(a)	Dunfermline Ath	D	1-1	Falconer	7,132
40		16	(a)	Morton	W	2-0	Nicholas C, Porteous	3,200
41		23	(h)	Hearts	D	0-0		10,500
42		30	(a)	Rangers	W	1-0	Irvine	36,010
43	May	4	(h)	Hibernian	L	0-2		7,000
44		7	(h)	Motherwell	D	0-0		5,500

FINAL LEAGUE POSITION: 4th in Premier Division

Appearances

Sub. Appearances

Goals

46

Appearance grid (player columns × match rows). Values are shirt numbers; `*` and `†` mark substitute/substituted appearances.

Leighton	McKimmie	Robertson	Simpson	McLeish	Miller W	Hackett	Grant	Miller J	Nicholas P	Hewitt	Connor	Dodds	Bett	Irvine	Falconer	Porteous	Edwards	Jones	Weir	Wright	Gray	Nicholas C	Gardner	McArthur	Harvie	#
1	2	3	4	5	6	7*	8†	9	10	11	12	14														1
1	2*	3	4	5	6	14	12	9†	10	11			7	8												2
1	2	3	4	5	6	14		9	10	11	7*	8	12													3
1	2	3	4		6			9	10	11	7	8	5													4
1	2	3	4*		6	11	12	9	10		7†	8	5	14												5
1	2	3			6	11†	12	9	10	7	4*	8	5	14												6
1	2	3		5	6	12		9	10	7*	4	8	11													7
1	2	3†		5	6	14		9	10	7	4	8	11*	12												8
1	2			5	14	3		9†	10	7*	4	8	6	11	12											9
1	2			5	6	3*		9	10	7	4	8	11	12												10
1	2			5	6			9	10	7	4	8	3*	11	12											11
1	2			5	6	11†	12			10	7	4	8	3	9*	14										12
1	2			5	6					10	7	4	8	3	9			11								13
1	2		4	5	6					10	7	3	8		9						11					14
1	2		4	5	6	14				10	7*	3	8		9†				12		11					15
1	2			5	6	14				10	7	3	8†		11	4*		9	12							16
1	2		4	5	6					10	9	11	7*	8	3			12								17
1	2	12		5	6					10*	9	4	7	8	3			11								18
1	2			5	6	12				11*	4	7	8		3			9	10							19
1	2			5	6	14				12	4	7	8		3			9*	10	11†						20
1	2			5	6					12	4	7	8		3			10	11	9*						21
1	2			5	6					10	14	4	7	8	3			12†	11*	9						22
1	2	3		5	6					10		4	7*	8	11			12		9						23
1	2	3		5	6					10	12	4	7†	8	11			14		9*						24
1	2	3		5	6					10	12	4	7	8	11*			14								25
1	2	3		5	6					10	12	4	7	8			11*	14		9†						26
1	2	3		5	6					10	12	4	7	8			11*	9†	14							27
1	2	3		5	6					10	11	4	7*	8			14	9	12							28
1	2	3		5	6					10	11*	4			9			12			8	7				29
1	2	3			6					10	11*	4	5		9			12			8	7				30
1	2	3*			6	11				10	12	4	8	5	9							7				31
1	2			5	6	11†				10	12	4	8	3*	9			14				7				32
1	2	3		5	6	12				10		4	7*	8†	11			14					9			33
1	2	3			6					10	12	4*	7		5			8			11		9			34
1	2	3			6					10		4*	8		5	12		7	14			11†	9			35
1	2		4	5	6					10		7	8		3			11					9			36
1	2		4	5	6					10		7	8		3			11					9			37
1	2		4	5	6					10	12	7	8		3			11*					9			38
1	2		4*	5	6					10†	11	7	8		3			12			14		9			39
1	2	3								11†	10		5	6	14		4		8		9*	7	12			40
1	2	3	5*		6					10		8	12	11			4				9		7			41
1		3	4	5	6					10			8				2	11	7				9			42
1				5	6					10	7†	12	8				2	11	4*			9		14	3	43
1	2		4	5	6					10	7	3	8					11					9			44
44	42	23	14	36	42	6	4	12	39	26	32	22	38	14	32	1	6	14	5	9	4	16	1	1	1	
	1							9	3	2	11	2	1	2	4	2	3	14		3		2				
1	1	3	1	4	3	1	1		9	10	1	8	1	2	3		4	3								

47

1988-89

1	Aug	13	(a)	Dundee	D	1-1	Dodds	12,222
2		20	(h)	St. Mirren	D	1-1	Connor	12,046
3		27	(a)	Dundee U	D	2-2	Bett (pen), Hewitt	14,735
4	Sep	3	(h)	Hibernian	D	0-0		13,583
5		17	(a)	Celtic	W	3-1	Grant, Bett (pen), Dodds	37,769
6		24	(h)	Hearts	W	1-0	Nicholas	14,000
7		27	(a)	Hamilton A	W	1-0	Connor	3,634
8	Oct	1	(a)	Motherwell	D	1-1	Miller	4,225
9		8	(h)	Rangers	W	2-1	Bett (pen), Nicholas	22,370
10		12	(a)	St. Mirren	D	1-1	Dodds	4,284
11		29	(a)	Hearts	D	1-1	Whittaker (og)	12,644
12	Nov	2	(h)	Celtic	D	2-2	Dodds, Nicholas	22,000
13		5	(a)	Hibernian	W	2-1	Nicholas 2	11,500
14		12	(h)	Dundee U	D	1-1	Mason	15,184
15		16	(h)	Dundee	W	1-0	Wright	11,181
16		19	(h)	Motherwell	W	2-1	Hewitt, Nicholas	10,028
17		26	(a)	Rangers	L	0-1		42,239
18	Dec	3	(h)	Hamilton A	D	1-1	Nicholas	8,324
19		10	(a)	Celtic	D	0-0		42,437
20		17	(h)	St. Mirren	W	3-1	Robertson C, Irvine, Hewitt	8,500
21		31	(a)	Dundee	L	0-2		9,828
22	Jan	3	(a)	Dundee U	D	1-1	Nicholas	17,952
23		7	(h)	Hibernian	W	2-0	Nicholas 2	13,500
24		14	(h)	Rangers	L	1-2	Nicholas	22,000
25		21	(a)	Motherwell	W	2-0	Van der Ark, Connor	5,906
26	Feb	14	(a)	Hamilton A	W	2-0	Connor, Wright	2,016
27		25	(h)	Hearts	W	3-0	Irvine, McPherson (og), Wright	15,000
28	Mar	11	(h)	Dundee	W	2-0	Nicholas, Wright	11,800
29		25	(a)	St. Mirren	W	3-1	Wright, Nicholas, Mason	7,541
30	Apr	1	(h)	Dundee U	W	1-0	Nicholas	16,700
31		8	(a)	Hibernian	W	2-1	Mason, Bett	11,000
32		15	(h)	Hamilton A	W	3-0	Mason, Nicholas 2	9,712
33		22	(a)	Hearts	L	0-1		13,367
34		29	(h)	Celtic	D	0-0		21,500
35	May	6	(h)	Motherwell	D	0-0		6,500
36		13	(a)	Rangers	W	3-0	Wright, Bett, Van der Ark	42,480

FINAL LEAGUE POSITION: 2nd in Premier Division

Appearances

Sub. Appearances

Goals

48

Snelders	McKimmie	Robertson D	Simpson	McLeish	Miller	Gray	Bett	Nicholas C	Connor	Hewitt	Dodds	Irvine	Mason	Wright	Grant	MacLeod	Robertson I	Robertson C	Van der Ark	Watson Gregg	Jess	No.
1	2	3	4	5	6	7	8	9*	10†	11	12	14										1
1	2	3	4	5	6		8		10	11			7*	9	12							2
1	2	3	4	5	6		8		10	11	9		7									3
1	2	3	4	5	6			12	10	11	9			8	7*							4
1	2	3		5	6		8	7	10	11*	9		12		4							5
1	2		4	5	6		8	7	10	11	9*		12		3							6
1	2	4*		5	6		8	7	10	11		3	12		9							7
1		3		5	6		8	7	10	11	9†	12	2*	14	4							8
1	2	3	4*	5	6		8	7	10	11	9	12										9
1	2	3	4	5	6		8	7*	10	11	9	12										10
1	2	3		5			8	7	10	12	9	6	4*		11							11
1	2	3		5			8	7	10	11†	9*	6	12	14	4							12
1	2	3		5			8	7	10		9	6	11		4							13
1	2	3			6		8	7*	10	12	9	5	11		4							14
1	2	3		5	6		8		10	7	9		11	12	4*							15
1	2	3		5	6		8	7	10	11*	9		4	12								16
1	2	3		5	6		8	7	10	11†	9	4*		14	12							17
1	2	3*	4	5	6		8	7	10	12	9†		11	14								18
1	2	3	4*	5		9		7	10	11		6	8		12							19
1	2	3		5		7			10	11	14	6	12	9*	4		8†					20
1	2	3*	4			7†			10	11	9	5	8	12	6			14				21
1	2		4	5			8	7*	10		14	6	11	9†	12			3				22
1	2		4	5			8	7	10	12		6	11*	9				3				23
1	2		4	5			8	7	10		12	6	11	9				3*				24
1	2		4	5			8	7	10	9†		6	12	14				3	11*			25
1	2		4	5			8	7	10	11		6		9				3				26
1	2	3*		5					10	11†	14	6	7	9	8		4		12			27
1	2			5	6		8	7	10	11				9	4		3					28
1	2*			5	6		8	7	10				12	11	9†	4	3		14			29
1	2			5	6		8	7	10	11†	14	12	3		4			9*				30
1	2			5	6	8*	7†		10	14		3	11	9	4				12			31
1	2			5	6		8	7	10			3	11	9	4*				12			32
1	2†			5	6		8	7	10	12		3	11*	9	4				14			33
1	2	3		5			8	7	10*			6	11	9†	4				14	12		34
1	2	3†		5			8	7	10			6	12		4				9	14	11*	35
1	2	3		5			8	7	10			6	11*	9†	4				7	12	14	36
36	35	23	16	34	21	4	31	28	36	21	17	21	21	15	22	1	7	2	4		1	
									1	6	6	6	7	8	4		2	4	4	1		
			1			5	16	4	3	4	2	4	6	1			1	2				

49

1989-90

1	Aug	12	(h)	Hibernian	W	1-0	Mason	16,000
2		19	(a)	Motherwell	D	0-0		6,491
3		26	(h)	Dundee	W	1-0	Jess	12,500
4	Sep	9	(a)	Rangers	L	0-1		40,283
5		16	(h)	Dunfermline Ath	W	2-1	Mason, Robertson C	13,000
6		23	(a)	St. Mirren	W	2-0	Mason, Grant	5,872
7		30	(h)	Celtic	D	1-1	McLeish	21,374
8	Oct	4	(a)	Dundee U	L	0-2		11,879
9		14	(h)	Hearts	L	1-3	Van der Ark	15,000
10		25	(a)	Hibernian	W	3-0	Robertson C, Mason, Van der Ark	12,000
11		28	(h)	Motherwell	W	1-0	Bett (pen)	13,500
12	Nov	4	(a)	Dundee	D	1-1	Connor	7,041
13		18	(a)	Dunfermline Ath	W	3-0	Gillhaus 2, Robertson D	11,882
14		22	(h)	Rangers	W	1-0	Gillhaus	23,000
15		25	(h)	St. Mirren	W	5-0	Nicholas 3, McLeish, Mason	13,500
16	Dec	2	(a)	Celtic	L	0-1		38,300
17		9	(h)	Dundee U	W	2-0	Nicholas, Mason	15,500
18		20	(a)	Hearts	D	1-1	Grant	11,370
19		26	(h)	Hibernian	L	1-2	Grant	16,500
20		30	(a)	Motherwell	D	2-2	Van der Ark 2	7,267
21	Jan	2	(h)	Dundee	W	5-2	Grant, Van der Ark 2, Bett, Nicholas	16,054
22		6	(a)	Rangers	L	0-2		41,351
23		13	(h)	Dunfermline Ath	W	4-1	Grant, Mason, Nicholas, Bett	14,000
24		27	(a)	St. Mirren	L	0-1		7,855
25	Feb	3	(h)	Hearts	D	2-2	Nicholas 2 (1 pen)	15,000
26		10	(a)	Dundee U	D	1-1	Mason	10,533
27		17	(h)	Celtic	D	1-1	Nicholas	22,100
28	Mar	3	(a)	Dunfermline Ath	W	4-2	Mason, Nicholas, Gillhaus 2	8,228
29		10	(a)	Hibernian	L	2-3	Van der Ark, Hunter (og)	9,500
30		24	(h)	Motherwell	W	2-0	Gillhaus 2	10,000
31		31	(a)	Dundee	D	1-1	Gillhaus	8,071
32	Apr	8	(h)	Rangers	D	0-0		23,000
33		18	(h)	Dundee U	W	1-0	Grant	10,000
34		21	(a)	Hearts	L	0-1		11,616
35		28	(h)	St. Mirren	W	2-0	Irvine, Nicholas	7,977
36	May	2	(a)	Celtic	W	3-1	Jess 2, Graham, Watson	20,154

FINAL LEAGUE POSITION: 2nd in Premier Division

Appearances

Sub. Appearances

Goals

Snelders	McKimmie	Robertson D	Grant	Irvine	Miller	Nicholas	Bett	Van der Ark	Connor	Mason	Dodds	Robertson C	Simpson	Cameron	McLeish	Jess	Robertson I	Harvie	Gillhaus	Watt	Watson Gregg	Minns	Watson Graham	Wright	Booth	No.
1	2	3	4	5	6	7	8	9*	10	11	12															1
1	2	3		5	6	7	8	9*	10	12			4	11												2
1	2	3	4†		6	7	8		10	9			14	12	5	11*										3
1	2	3	4		6	7	8	11*	10	9		12			5											4
1	2	3			6	7	8	12	10	9		4			5	11*										5
1	2	3	4		6	7	8	12	10	9				11*	5											6
1	2		4*	12	6	7	8		14	10	9		3	11†	5											7
1	2		4	12	6	7	8	11	10	9†		3*		14	5											8
1	2	3	12		6	7*	8	14	10	9		4		11†	5											9
1	2	3		6		14	8*		7	9		4			5	11†	10	12								10
1	2	3*		12	6	7	8	11	10	9		4			5											11
1	2		12	3	6		8	7	10	9		4*			5	11										12
1	2	3	4	6		7	8*	14	10	9		12			5				11†							13
1	2	3	4	6		7*	8	12	10	9					5				11							14
1	2	3*	4	6		7	8	14	10	9†		12			5				11							15
1	2	3	4*	6		7†	8	14	10	9		12			5				11							16
1	2	3	4	6		7	8	12	10*	9					5				11							17
1	2	3	4	6		7	8		10	9					5				11							18
	2	3	4*	6		7	8	14	10	9		12			5				11†	1						19
	2		4	6		7		11*	10	9		12	8	3	5					1						20
	2		4	6		7	8	11	10†	9*			12		5	14				1	3					21
	2		4	6		7†	8	11	10	9		14	12		5				3*	1						22
	2	3	4*	6		7	8	11†	10	9			12		5	14				1						23
	2		4	6		7†		11	10	9		12	8		5		3*		14	1						24
1	2		4	6		7		11	10						5		3		9		8					25
	2		4	6		7		8	10	9			12		5		3		11*	1						26
	2		4	6		7	8†		10	9		12		14	5		3*		11			1				27
	2		4	3	6	7	8		10	9					5				11			1				28
	2		4*	3†	6	7	8	14	10	9		12			5				11			1				29
	2		12	6		7	8*	10†		9		4		14	5		3		11			1				30
	2		4	6		7	8	10*	3	9		12			5				11			1				31
	2		4	6		7	8		3	9		10*	12		5				11			1				32
1		3	4	6		7	8		10	9†					5	14			11		2*		12			33
1		3	4	6			8*		10	9		12			5	7			11				2			34
1			4	5	6	7*			10	9		2			8				11				3†	12	14	35
1	2	3		5	6							7	8	11	10						12	4*		9		36
23	33	20	28	28	15	32	30	15	34	33		10	5	6	32	7	5	1	19	7	3	6	3		1	
		3	3	1		11		1	1	12	4	5		4		1	1	1		1	1	1				
		1	6	1		11	3	7	1	9		2			2	3		8				1				

1990-91

1	Aug	25	(h)	Hibernian	W	2-0	Gillhaus, Connor	15,500
2	Sep	1	(a)	Celtic	W	3-0	Mason, Connor, Gillhaus	45,222
3		8	(a)	Dunfermline Ath	D	1-1	Robertson D	10,200
4		15	(h)	Dundee U	D	1-1	Bett (pen)	15,500
5		22	(h)	St. Mirren	W	2-1	Irvine, Bett	12,500
6		29	(a)	St. Johnstone	L	0-5		8,711
7	Oct	6	(h)	Rangers	D	0-0		24,000
8		13	(a)	Motherwell	D	0-0		6,602
9		20	(h)	Hearts	W	3-0	Bett, Grant, Gillhaus	14,800
10		27	(a)	Hibernian	D	1-1	Gillhaus	10,500
11	Nov	3	(h)	Celtic	W	3-0	Jess 2, Gillhaus	21,500
12		10	(a)	St. Mirren	W	4-0	Grant, Robertson C, Jess, Gillhaus	7,638
13		17	(h)	St. Johnstone	D	0-0		16,000
14		24	(a)	Dundee U	W	3-2	Jess 3	12,344
15	Dec	1	(h)	Dunfermline Ath	W	3-2	Irvine, Gillhaus, Mason	12,000
16		8	(a)	Hearts	L	0-1		9,811
17		15	(h)	Motherwell	D	1-1	Jess	9,500
18		22	(a)	Rangers	D	2-2	Bett 2 (1 pen)	37,998
19		26	(h)	St. Mirren	W	1-0	Jess	8,755
20	Jan	2	(h)	Dundee U	L	0-1		19,000
21		5	(a)	Dunfermline Ath	W	4-1	Jess 4	7,422
22		12	(h)	Hibernian	W	2-0	Cameron, Booth	13,500
23		19	(a)	Celtic	L	0-1		28,187
24	Feb	2	(h)	Hearts	W	5-0	Connor, Booth 2, Mason, Gillhaus	9,500
25		13	(a)	St. Johnstone	W	1-0	Booth	7,046
26	Mar	2	(h)	Rangers	W	1-0	Gillhaus	22,500
27		5	(a)	Motherwell	W	2-0	Wright, Bett	5,567
28		13	(h)	Dunfermline Ath	D	0-0		10,400
29		23	(a)	Dundee U	W	2-1	Van der Ark, Gillhaus	10,643
30		30	(a)	Hibernian	W	4-2	Gillhaus 3, Booth	7,400
31	Apr	6	(h)	Celtic	W	1-0	Jess	22,500
32		13	(a)	Hearts	W	4-1	Gillhaus, McKimmie, Connor 2	16,771
33		20	(h)	Motherwell	W	3-0	Van der Ark 2, Connor	14,500
34		27	(a)	St. Mirren	W	1-0	Bett	8,513
35	May	4	(h)	St. Johnstone	W	2-1	Van der Ark, Booth	18,000
36		11	(a)	Rangers	L	0-2		37,652

FINAL LEAGUE POSITION: 2nd in Premier Division

Appearances

Sub. Appearances

Goals

Snelders	McKimmie	Robertson D	Grant	McLeish	Irvine	Van de Ven	Bett	Mason	Connor	Gillhaus	Watson Gregg	Jess	Booth	Wright	Robertson C	Dibble	Cameron	Robertson I	Watt	Van der Ark	
1	2	3	4	5	6	7	8*	9	10	11	12										1
1	2*	3	4	5	6	7	8	9	10	11	12										2
1	2	3	4	5	6	7	8	9	10	11											3
1	2	3	4	5	6	7*	8	9	10	11†		12	14								4
1		3	4	5	6	7	8	9		11		2	10								5
1	2	3	4		6	7*	8	9	10	11†		5	14		12						6
1†	2		4	5	6	3	8	9	10	11		12	7*		14						7
	2	3	4	5	6	7	8	9	10	11					1						8
	2	3	4	5	6	7	8*	9	10	11†		12		14	1						9
	2	3	4	5	6	7*	8	9†	10	11		14		12	1						10
	2	3	4	5	6	7	8		10*	11		9		1	12						11
	2	3	4†		6*	7	8		10	11		9	5	1	14	12					12
	2	3		5	6	7	8		10	11*		9	4		12	1					13
	2	3		5	6	7	8	9	10	11		4*			12	1					14
	2	3		5	6	7	8	9*	10	11		4			12	1					15
		3		5	6	7	8	9	10	11*		4†	2	12	14	1					16
1	2	3	4	5		7	8	9*	10	11		6†	14	12							17
1	2	3	4	5	6	7	8	9		11		10									18
1	2	3	4	5	6	7*	8	9		11†		10			14	12					19
1	2*	3	4	5	6	7	8	9		11†		10			14	12					20
1	2	3	4	5	6		8	9		11		10		7							21
1		3	4	5	6		8	9		11		10*	12	7				2			22
1		3	4	5	6	7*	8	9		11		12			10			2			23
1		3	4	5	6	12	8*	14	10	11		7	9†					2			24
1		3	4	5	6		8	9	10	11*		12		7				2			25
1		3	4*	5	6	12	8	9†	10	11		7						2		14	26
1		3	4	5	6	12	8	9†	10	11		7*						2		14	27
1		3	4	5	6†		8	9*	10	11		12		7				2		14	28
1		3	4	5	6	12	8		10	11		7†	14					2		9*	29
1†	6	3	4	5*		12	8		10	11		14		7				2		9	30
	6	3	4	5		7†	8		10	11		9*	14					2	1	12	31
	6	3	4	5		12	8		10	11†		7	14					2*	1	9	32
	6	3	4	5*		12	8		10	11†		7	14					2	1	9	33
	6	3	4	5		12	8		10	11		7†	14					2	1	9*	34
	6	3	4	5		12	8		10	11		14		7†				2	1	9*	35
	6	3	4	5		7*	8		10	11		9†	14					2	1	12	36
21	26	35	32	33	29	23	36	25	29	35	2	20	8	16	2	5	3	10	6		
							9	1				5	7	11	1	6		7	1	5	
	1		2	2			7	3	6	14		13	6	1	1	1		1		4	

53

1991-92

#	Month	Date		Opponent	Res	Score	Scorers	Attendance
1	Aug	10	(a)	Airdrieonians	W	2-1	Irvine, Gillhaus	6,337
2		14	(a)	Falkirk	W	1-0	Booth	8,462
3		17	(h)	Dunfermline Ath	W	3-1	Bett, Grant, Jess	13,849
4		24	(h)	Celtic	W	1-0	Gillhaus	20,503
5		31	(a)	Dundee U	D	0-0		11,964
6	Sep	7	(h)	St. Johnstone	L	1-2	Van de Ven	12,071
7		14	(a)	Motherwell	W	1-0	Gillhaus	6,452
8		21	(h)	Hibernian	D	1-1	Grant	11,850
9		28	(a)	Rangers	W	2-0	Jess, Grant	36,330
10	Oct	5	(h)	St. Mirren	W	4-1	Ten Caat, Grant, Irvine, Mason	10,154
11		9	(a)	Hearts	L	0-1		15,569
12		12	(h)	Airdrieonians	W	3-1	Ten Caat, Jess 2	8,998
13		19	(a)	Dunfermline Ath	D	0-0		5,157
14		26	(a)	St. Johnstone	W	3-1	Van de Ven, Jess, Mason	5,682
15		30	(h)	Motherwell	W	3-1	Winnie, Mason, Gillhaus	9,092
16	Nov	2	(h)	Dundee U	L	0-1		13,728
17		9	(a)	Celtic	L	1-2	Jess	36,837
18		16	(a)	St. Mirren	W	1-0	McIntyre (og)	3,634
19		20	(h)	Hearts	L	0-2		15,338
20		23	(a)	Hibernian	L	0-1		8,942
21		30	(h)	Falkirk	D	1-1	Gillhaus	10,614
22	Dec	4	(h)	Rangers	L	2-3	Ten Caat, Irvine	20,081
23		7	(a)	Airdrieonians	L	0-2		3,071
24		14	(h)	St. Johnstone	W	4-1	Jess, Grant, Booth, Roddie	9,292
25		28	(h)	Celtic	D	2-2	Ten Caat, Jess	20,422
26	Jan	1	(a)	Dundee U	L	0-4		7,777
27		4	(h)	St. Mirren	D	0-0		8,774
28		11	(a)	Hearts	W	4-0	Jess 2, Booth, Mason	16,291
29		14	(a)	Motherwell	D	3-3	Kane, Jess, Roddie	5,221
30		18	(a)	Falkirk	D	2-2	Mason, Booth	5,122
31	Feb	1	(h)	Dunfermline Ath	D	1-1	Jess	7,549
32		8	(h)	Hibernian	L	0-1		9,568
33		25	(a)	Rangers	D	0-0		36,513
34		29	(a)	St. Mirren	W	2-0	Mason, Smith	3,853
35	Mar	14	(a)	Celtic	L	0-1		29,380
36		18	(h)	Hearts	W	2-0	Ten Caat, Mason	10,581
37		21	(h)	Dundee U	L	0-2		10,350
38		28	(h)	Airdrieonians	W	1-0	Irvine	6,805
39	Apr	4	(a)	Dunfermline Ath	D	0-0		3,033
40		8	(a)	St. Johnstone	D	0-0		4,524
41		11	(h)	Motherwell	W	2-0	Grant, Kane	6,902
42		18	(a)	Hibernian	D	1-1	Paatelainen	6,777
43		25	(h)	Falkirk	D	1-1	Booth	6,461
44	May	2	(h)	Rangers	L	0-2		16,580

FINAL LEAGUE POSITION: 6th in Premier Division

Appearances

Sub. Appearances

Goals

54

Snelders	Wright	Connor	Grant	Irvine	McKimmie	Van de Ven	Bett	Jess	Ten Caat	Gillhaus	Winnie	Booth	Watson Greg	Van der Ark	Cameron	Mason	Watson Grah.	Gibson	Roddie	Smith	Kane	Watt	McLeish	Ferguson	Humphries	Paatelainen	
1	2	3	4	5	6	7	8	9†	10*	11	12	14															1
1	2	10	4	5	6	7†	8	14		11	3	9*	12														2
1	2	10	4	5	6	12	8	14		11	3	9*		7†													3
1	2		4	5	6	7	8			11	3	14	12	9*	10†												4
1	2	10	4*	5	6	12	8	9†		11	3	14				7											5
1	2*	10		5	6	4	8		12	11	3	9		14		7†											6
1	2	3	4	5	6	12	8			10*	11		14	9		7†											7
1	2		4	5	6	7	8			10*	11	3†	14		12	9											8
1		3	4	5	6	7†	8	11*	10			9		12	2	14											9
1		3	4	5†	6	7	8	11	10			9*		12	2	14											10
1		3	4	5	6	7*	8	11	10			9†		12	2	14											11
1		3	4†	5	6	7	8	11	10			9*		12	2		14										12
1		3	4*		6		8	11	10	14	5	9†		12	7	2											13
1				5	6	2	8	4	10	11†	3	9*	14	12	7												14
1				5	6	2	8	4*	10	11	3	9†	14	12	7												15
1				5	6	2	8	9	10	11†	3	14	4	12	7*												16
1				5		7	8	4*	10	11	3	9	6	12		2†	14										17
1				5	6	7	8	4	10	11*	3	12	2	9		14											18
1				5	6	7*	8	4	10	11	3	12		9†		14		2									19
1				5	6	7	8	11	10		3	9		12	2			4*									20
				6		7	8	10†		11	3	9		12			14	2	4*	1	5						21
1				6		7*	8	12	10†	11	3	14	9	4			2		5								22
1		4		6		7	8	14		11*	3		9	10†			2	12	5								23
1		4*	5		7	8	11	10		9†			3	14	2	6			12								24
1		4	6	2		8	7	10		9†	12				14	3	11*	6									25
1		4		6		8	11	10†	14	9	3*		7			2	12	5									26
1		4	6	2		10		11	9†			7		14	3	8	5										27
1		4†	6	2		10		11	3	9		7		14	12	8	5*										28
1	6		5	2		8	10	11	3	9†		7*		14	4		12										29
1	6	4	5	2		8	10	11	3	12		7		9*													30
1	6	4	5	2		10		11	12†		7		9*	3	8		14										31
1	6	4	5	2		11	10†	14		9	7		3	8													32
1	6	4	5	2		8	11	10	7†		14		3	8													33
	6	4	5	2		8	11	10	12	7*		3	9	1													34
1	6	4	5	2		8	11	10†		7	14		3	9													35
1	6	4	5	2		8	11	10	14	7		3	9†														36
1	6	4	5	2		8	9†	10	11*	7		3	12		14												37
1		4	5	2		8	11	10	6	7		3	9														38
1	6	4		2		8	10	12	5	7*		9					3	11									39
1	6	4	5	2		10†		14	8	7		9					3	11									40
1	6	4	5	2		8	7*	10	3	12	14	9					11										41
1	6	4	5	2		8	12	3	7	10*	14	9†					11										42
1	6	4	5	2		8	10*	3	14	12	7†	9					11										43
1	6	4	5	2		12	10	3	9	7†	14	9					11*										44
42	23	11	33	41	39	20	38	33	28	24	27	21	4	7	4	28	4	2	1	15	22	2	7	2	6		
					3		6	2	5	1	12	6	11	2	3	5	3	9	1	3			4				
		6	4		2	1	12	5	5	1	5				7			2	1	2			1				

55

1992-93

1	Aug	1	(h)	Hibernian	W	3-0	Shearer 2, Booth	12,503
2		5	(h)	Celtic	D	1-1	Shearer	14,618
3		8	(a)	Falkirk	W	1-0	Aitken	5,925
4		15	(a)	Motherwell	L	1-2	Jess	5,561
5		22	(h)	Dundee	W	2-1	Shearer, Paatelainen	11,604
6		29	(a)	Rangers	L	1-3	Aitken	41,636
7	Sep	2	(h)	Airdrieonians	D	0-0		9,021
8		12	(a)	Hearts	L	0-1		10,630
9		19	(h)	Partick Thistle	W	2-0	Grant, Paatelainen	9,755
10		26	(a)	St. Johnstone	W	3-0	Shearer 2, Paatelainen	7,320
11	Oct	3	(h)	Dundee U	L	0-1		12,936
12		7	(a)	Hibernian	W	3-1	Shearer, Jess 2	8,824
13		17	(h)	Falkirk	W	3-1	Jess, Paatelainen, Booth	9,016
14		31	(a)	Airdrieonians	W	2-1	Sandison (og), Shearer	3,221
15	Nov	7	(a)	Dundee	W	2-1	Shearer, Richardson	6,902
16		11	(h)	Motherwell	W	2-0	Shearer, Grant	8,725
17		24	(a)	Partick Thistle	W	7-0	Shearer 3, Jess, Mason, Booth, Kane	3,986
18		28	(h)	Hearts	W	6-2	Irvine, Shearer 3, Mason, Booth	13,555
19	Dec	2	(a)	Celtic	D	2-2	Jess, Kane	29,122
20		5	(h)	St. Johnstone	W	3-0	Irvine, Roddie, Mason	11,750
21		12	(a)	Dundee U	D	2-2	Jess, Irvine	10,394
22		19	(h)	Hibernian	W	2-0	Richardson, Booth	11,018
23		26	(a)	Motherwell	W	2-0	Irvine, Jess	7,907
24	Jan	2	(h)	Dundee	D	0-0		13,201
25		16	(h)	Airdrieonians	W	7-0	Paatelainen 4, Jess, Booth, Irvine	8,805
26		30	(a)	Falkirk	W	4-1	Jess 2, Shearer, Booth	6,886
27	Feb	2	(h)	Rangers	L	0-1		15,055
28		13	(h)	Celtic	D	1-1	Paatelainen	14,673
29		20	(a)	St. Johnstone	W	2-0	Jess, Booth	6,176
30		24	(h)	Dundee U	D	0-0		12,603
31	Mar	2	(h)	Partick Thistle	W	1-0	Paatelainen	8,287
32		9	(a)	Hibernian	W	2-1	Kane, Paatelainen	7,029
33		13	(h)	Falkirk	D	2-2	Roddie, Shearer	9,095
34		20	(a)	Dundee	W	2-1	Paatelainen, Booth	5,783
35		27	(h)	Motherwell	W	1-0	Booth	9,155
36		30	(a)	Rangers	L	0-2		44,270
37	Apr	10	(a)	Airdrieonians	D	1-1	Shearer	3,005
38		17	(h)	Hearts	W	3-2	Shearer, Paatelainen, Mason	9,700
39		20	(a)	Partick Thistle	W	3-1	Paatelainen 2, Kane	3,445
40	May	1	(a)	Celtic	L	0-1		20,642
41		5	(a)	Hearts	W	2-1	Shearer, Paatelainen	6,038
42		8	(h)	St. Johnstone	D	1-1	Booth	7,727
43		12	(h)	Rangers	W	1-0	Shearer	13,079
44		15	(a)	Dundee U	W	4-1	Booth 2, Gibson, Grant	9,078

FINAL LEAGUE POSITION: 2nd in Premier Division

Appearances

Sub. Appearances

Goals

Snelders	Wright	Winnie	Aitken	Irvine	Smith	Mason	Bett	Booth	Shearer	Paatelainen	Jess	Ferguson	McKimmie	Thomson	Roddie	Kane	Grant	McLeish	Ten Caat	Richardson	Watt	Connor	Gibson	
1	2	3	4	5	6	7	8	9	10*	11	12													1
1	2	3	4	5	6	7	8	9*	10	11	12													2
1	12	3	4	5	6	7*	8		10	11	9		2											3
1	8	3†	4	5	6	7			10*	11	9	12	2	14										4
1	3	12	4	5	6		8*		10	11	9		2	14		7†								5
1	3	12	4	5	6	7*			10	11	9		2	14		8								6
1	3†	10	4	5	6	7				11	9		2	14		8								7
1	14	3	4	5	6	12	8*		10	11†	9		2			7								8
1	2	3			6	7			10	11	9						4	5	8†	14				9
	2	3			6	12			10	11	9					7	4	5†	14	8	1			10
1	2	3		5	6	12			10	11	9					14	4		7†	8*				11
1	2	3		5	6	7			10†	11*	9					14	12	4		8				12
1	2	3	7		6	12		14	10†	11	9						4*	5		8				13
1	2	3		5	6		8		10	11	9					12	4			7				14
1	2	3		5	6	12	8		10	11	9						4*			7				15
1	2	3		5	6	12	8		10*	11	9						4			7				16
1	2		5	6	11	8†	14	10			9					12	4	3		7*				17
1	2*		5	6	11	8†	14	10			9					12	4	3		7				18
1	2		5	6	11	8	10†				9*			14		12	4	3		7				19
1	2		5	6	11	8	9								10		4	3		7				20
1	2		5	6	11	8†	10				9					12	4	3		7				21
1	2†	14	5	6	11	8	10*				9					12	4	3		7				22
1	2		5	6	11	8	10				9					14	4	3		7†				23
1	2		5	6	11	8	10				9						4	3		7				24
1	2	12	5	3	8				10†	11	9					14	4	6		7*				25
1	2	12	5	3	11		8		10†		9					14	4	6		7*				26
1	2		5	3	11†		8	12	10		9					14	4	6		7†				27
1	2	3	8	5				14	10†	11	9						4	6		7				28
	2	12	5	3	8			14	10†	11	9						4	6		7	1			29
1	2	4	5	3	8			14	10†	11	9							6		7				30
1	2	12	5	3	14		8		10†	11	9						4	6		7				31
1	2	8	5	3					10†	11						14	12	4	6	9	7*			32
1	2	3†	8	5					10	11						14	7	4	6	9				33
1	2	8	5	3	14			9	12	11*			6				7	4		10†				34
1	2			3	8			9		11			6			14	4†	5	10	7				35
1	2	3	8†					9	10	11			6			14	4	5	12	7*				36
1	12		5	3	8			9†	10	11			2			14	4	6		7*				37
1	4		5	3	8			9†	10	11			2			14		6		7				38
1			5	3	8	8	14		10†	11			2				4	6		7*	12			39
1	4		5			7†	14		10	11			2			12	8	6	9*			3		40
	4		5			7*		9	10	11			2				8	6	12		1	3		41
1	2	12	5	6	8			9	10†	11							4*		14	7		3		42
1	2	12	5	6	8			9	10								4		11*	7		3		43
1	2	12	5	6	8			9	14								4	7	11†			3	10	44
41	34	18	18	39	40	31	17	21	32	33	28		14		1	13	29	27	11	28	3	5	1	
	2	3	8		3		3	2		3	1		2	10	14		4			1				
		2	5		4		13	22	16	12						2	4	3		2		1		

57

1993-94

#	Month	Date		Opponent	Res	Score	Scorers	Att
1	Aug	7	(a)	Dundee U	D	1-1	Booth	13,881
2		14	(h)	Kilmarnock	W	1-0	Kane	13,535
3		21	(a)	Dundee	D	1-1	Shearer	7,505
4		28	(h)	St. Johnstone	D	0-0		11,682
5	Sep	4	(a)	Celtic	W	1-0	Paatelainen	34,311
6		11	(a)	Hibernian	L	1-2	Shearer	8,506
7		18	(h)	Rangers	W	2-0	Shearer, Pressley (og)	19,138
8		25	(h)	Raith R	W	4-1	Shearer, Jess, Richardson 2	11,472
9	Oct	2	(a)	Motherwell	D	0-0		8,597
10		5	(h)	Hearts	D	0-0		13,798
11		9	(a)	Partick Thistle	L	2-3	Paatelainen, Shearer	5,600
12		16	(a)	Kilmarnock	D	1-1	Paatelainen	9,108
13		23	(h)	Dundee U	W	2-0	Paatelainen, Shearer	13,566
14		30	(h)	Dundee	W	1-0	Shearer	11,885
15	Nov	6	(a)	St. Johnstone	D	1-1	Booth	5,757
16		9	(h)	Celtic	D	1-1	Grant (og)	19,474
17		13	(h)	Motherwell	D	1-1	Booth	12,494
18		27	(h)	Hibernian	W	4-0	Kane, Connor, Shearer, Grant	12,334
19	Dec	1	(a)	Rangers	L	0-2		45,182
20		4	(a)	Hearts	D	1-1	Shearer	9,402
21		7	(a)	Raith R	D	1-1	Miller	4,205
22		14	(h)	Partick Thistle	W	2-1	Irvine, Shearer	8,248
23		18	(h)	Kilmarnock	W	3-1	Miller, Shearer, Richardson	10,834
24		27	(a)	Dundee U	W	1-0	Jess	12,248
25	Jan	8	(h)	St. Johnstone	D	1-1	Shearer	12,712
26		11	(a)	Dundee	W	1-0	Irvine	5,219
27		19	(a)	Celtic	D	2-2	Irvine, Jess	19,083
28		22	(h)	Rangers	D	0-0		20,267
29	Feb	5	(a)	Hibernian	L	1-3	Richardson	9,556
30		12	(h)	Raith R	W	4-0	Paatelainen 2, Shearer, Booth	10,553
31	Mar	5	(h)	Hearts	L	0-1		13,059
32		8	(a)	Motherwell	D	1-1	Shearer	7,018
33		19	(a)	Kilmarnock	W	3-2	Miller, Shearer, Jess	8,544
34		26	(h)	Dundee U	W	1-0	Shearer	12,574
35		29	(h)	Hibernian	L	2-3	Jess, Miller	10,832
36	Apr	2	(a)	Rangers	D	1-1	Kane	45,888
37		5	(a)	Partick Thistle	D	1-1	Tierney (og)	4,280
38		16	(h)	Motherwell	D	0-0		9,642
39		23	(h)	Partick Thistle	W	2-0	Jess, Grant	7,827
40		27	(a)	Hearts	D	1-1	Irvine	13,811
41		30	(h)	Dundee	D	1-1	Irvine	7,568
42	May	3	(a)	Raith R	W	2-0	Roddie, Shearer	2,798
43		7	(a)	St. Johnstone	W	1-0	Irvine	6,107
44		14	(h)	Celtic	D	1-1	Irvine	16,417

FINAL LEAGUE POSITION: 2nd in Premier Division

Appearances

Sub. Appearances

Goals

58

Snelders	McKimmie	Connor	Grant	Irvine	Smith	Richardson	Bett	Booth	Jess	Paatelainen	Shearer	Kane	McLeish	Miller	Wright	Aitken	Ten Caat	Winnie	Gibson	Watt	Roddie	Stillie	Robertson	Burridge	McKinnon	Thomson	No.
1	2	3	4	5	6	7	8	9	10*	11	12																1
1	2	3		6	7	8*	9	14	11†	10	4	5	12														2
1	2	14		6	7			9	11	10	4	5	8†	3	12												3
1	2		6	3	8			9	7†	12	10	4	5	14			11										4
1	2	3	6		7*	8	9	14	12	10†	4	5	11														5
1	2	3*	6			8		9†	11	10	4	5	7					12	14								6
1	2	11	6		8		14	9*	12	10†	4	5	7	3													7
1	2	11	6		8			9	14	10	4	5†	7	3*				12									8
1	2	11†	6	14	8			9*	12	10	4	5	7	3													9
1	2	11	6		8			14	10	4	5	7	3*					12	9†								10
	2†	12	6	14		8		9	11	10	4	5	7	3*								1					11
1	2	12	8	6	3	7		14	9†	11	10*	4	5														12
1	2		8†	6	3	7			9	11	10	4	5	12	14												13
1	2	12	8*	6	3	7		14	9	11	10†	4	5														14
1	2	3	8	6		7*		14	9	11	10†	4			12												15
1	2	3	8*	6		7		9	10		12	4		11	5			14									16
	2	3	8	6		7		9		11	14	4		10	5							1					17
1	2	11	8	6				9		10	4	5	7	3													18
	2†	11	8	6		14		9	12	10	4	5	7*	3								1					19
1		11	8†	6	3	14		10	9	12	4	5	7*	2													20
1		3	8	6		11†		9	14	12	10*	4	5	7	2												21
1		11	8†	6	3			14	9	12	10	4	5	7*	2												22
1		11†		6	3	8		14	9	12	10	4	5	7*	2												23
1	2	11		6				14	9†	12	10*	4	5	7	3			8									24
1	2*	11	12	6				14	9		10	4	5	7	3			8†									25
1	2	11	8	6				9	7†		10	4	5		3			12			14						26
	2		8	6		11		14	9†		10	4	5	7*	3			12	1								27
1	2		8*	6		11		14	9	12	10	4	5	7†	3												28
1	2	11†	4	6		8		9	7	14	10		5		3												29
1	2		4	6			8†	14	7	11	10	9	5		3												30
1†	2		4	6		8		9		12	10	11	5	7	3								14				31
	2		12	6	4	8		9†	7	14	10*	11	5		3							1					32
	2			6	4	8			7†	14	10	11	5	9	3							1					33
	2		12	6		8			7	14	10†	4	5	9	3*						11			1			34
	2			6		8			7	14	10	4	5†	9	3						11			1			35
	2		11	6		8			7	12	10*	4	5		3				9					1			36
	2		11	6		8			7	10		4	5		3				9†				3	1		14	37
1	2		12	6	3	8		9	7		10	4	5		11												38
1	2		8	6	5	14		9*	7	12	10	4			3†										11		39
1	2		8	6	5			9*	7	12	10				3				14		11		4†				40
1	2		4	6	5	8*			7	11	10†				3				12	9					14		41
1	2		4	6	5	8			7*	12	10				3				11†	9					14		42
1	2		4	6	5	12			7*		10	8			3				11	14			9†				43
	2		4	6	5	8†			7		10	9			3				11	14	1						44
33	40	21	26	42	19	31	6	14	38	14	39	39	35	24	34	1	2	1	4	3	4	6	3	5			
	4	4		2	4			11	3	22	4		3	2	1		2	4	1			3	1	2		3	
	1	2	7			4	6	6	17	3		4					1		4								

59

1994-95

1	Aug	13	(h)	Hearts	W	3-1	Robertson, Dodds, Booth	14,238
2		20	(h)	Falkirk	D	2-2	Robertson, Booth	11,143
3		27	(a)	Dundee U	L	1-2	Grant	9,332
4	Sep	10	(a)	Hibernian	D	2-2	Dodds, Grant	9,728
5		17	(h)	Partick Thistle	D	1-1	Dodds	10,425
6		24	(h)	Rangers	D	2-2	Booth, Dodds	19,191
7	Oct	1	(a)	Kilmarnock	L	1-2	Booth	7,445
8		8	(a)	Celtic	D	0-0		29,454
9		15	(h)	Motherwell	L	1-3	Dodds	12,489
10		22	(a)	Hearts	L	0-2		10,655
11		29	(h)	Dundee U	W	3-0	Kane 2, Booth	11,744
12	Nov	5	(a)	Falkirk	L	1-2	Booth	6,185
13		9	(h)	Hibernian	D	0-0		10,882
14		19	(a)	Partick Thistle	L	1-2	Dodds	3,795
15		25	(a)	Rangers	L	0-1		45,072
16	Dec	3	(h)	Kilmarnock	L	0-1		10,345
17		10	(a)	Motherwell	W	1-0	McCart (og)	7,020
18		26	(h)	Celtic	D	0-0		19,206
19		31	(h)	Hearts	W	3-1	Shearer 2, Inglis	11,392
20	Jan	2	(a)	Dundee U	D	0-0		10,560
21		7	(h)	Falkirk	D	0-0		14,141
22		14	(h)	Partick Thistle	W	3-1	Dinnie (og), Jess, Shearer	9,833
23		21	(a)	Hibernian	L	2-4	Dodds 2	8,076
24	Feb	4	(a)	Kilmarnock	L	1-3	McKimmie	9,384
25		12	(h)	Rangers	W	2-0	Dodds, Shearer	18,060
26		25	(h)	Motherwell	L	0-2		10,319
27	Mar	5	(a)	Celtic	L	0-2		20,621
28		11	(a)	Partick Thistle	D	2-2	Wright, Dodds	6,886
29		18	(h)	Hibernian	D	0-0		10,384
30	Apr	1	(h)	Kilmarnock	L	0-1		14,041
31		8	(a)	Rangers	L	2-3	Dodds, Shearer	44,460
32		15	(h)	Celtic	W	2-0	Shearer, Irvine	16,668
33		18	(a)	Motherwell	L	1-2	Dodds	7,155
34		29	(a)	Hearts	W	2-1	Dodds 2	11,466
35	May	6	(h)	Dundee U	W	2-1	Dodds, Shearer	20,124
36		13	(a)	Falkirk	W	2-0	Thomson, Glass	12,835

FINAL LEAGUE POSITION: 9th in Premier Division

Appearances

Sub. Appearances

Goals

Promotion/Relegation Play-Off

	May	21	(h)	Dunfermline Ath	W	3-1	Glass, Shearer 2	21,000
		25	(a)	Dunfermline Ath	W	3-1	Dodds, Miller, Glass	16,000

Snelders	McKimmie	Winnie	Grant	Irvine	Wright	Jess	Shearer	Kane	Dodds	Robertson	Hetherston	Booth	Miller	Woodthorpe	McKinnon	Smith	Watt	Glass	Inglis	Thomson	Aitken	Kpedekpo	
1	2	3	4	5	6	7	8†	9	10	11	12	14											1
1	2	3	4	5†	6	14	8	9	10	11		7	12										2
1	2		4	5	6	7	8†	9	10				14	3	11								3
1	2	11	4		6	7			10				9	3	8	5							4
	2		4	5	6	7			10				9†	14	3	11	8	1					5
	2		4	5	6	7			10†		12		9	14	3	11*	8	1					6
	2	8	4	5	6				10			7	9	12	3	11		1					7
	2		4	5	6		8		10				9	3	11	7		1					8
	2		4	5	6		8		10		11†		9	14	3	7		1					9
	2	12	4	5*	6		8		10		14	11†	9	3		7		1					10
1	2	5	4*		6		8		10		12		9	3		11†	7		14				11
1	2	5	4		6	12	8		10				9	3†		11*	7		14				12
1	2	14	4				8†		10				9	3	11	5			6	7			13
1	2	14	4				8		10†		12		9	3	11*	5			6	7			14
1	2†	8			6	11*			4		10	12		3		7			14	5	9		15
1	2	8*		7*	6				4		10	12	9	3†		11			5	14			16
1	2	8			3				4		10		6	9		7			11	5			17
1	2	8			3	14			4		10†	12	6	9†		7			11*	5			18
1	2	11			3		8		4		10		9			7			12	6	5		19
1	2*	7			3	14	8†		4		10		9			11			6	5	12		20
1		7			3	14	8		4		10		9			11†	2		6	5			21
1	2	11			3†	7	8		4		10		9			6		14		5	12		22
1	2	11				7	8*		4		10		9†	14		6			3	5			23
1	2	8			3	14			4*		10		9			6	11		5	7	12		24
1	2†				3	7	8		4		10		9			11			6	14	5		25
1		5	2			7	8†		4		10		12	9*		11†		6	15	3	14		26
	2	4†	5		3	7			10		12	14	9			11		6	1	8			27
1	2	4	5		3	14			10		12		9			11†	6		8	7			28
1†	2	11			3	12	8		4		10†		7			9†	6	15		5	14		29
	2	11†			3	14	8		4		10		7			9		1	6	5			30
	2	11†			3	14	8		4		10		7			9		1	6	5			31
	2	11	5		3	12	8		4		10†		7			9†		1	6	14			32
	2	11*	5		3	12	8		4		10		7			9		1	6†	14			33
	2	11	4	5	3		8		10		12		7			9*		1	6†	14			34
1	2		4	5	3		8		10			11*	7			9			6	14			35
1	2		4	5	3		8		10				9			11	7		6	14			36
24	34	6	32	17	33	15	19	27	35	2	13	11	21	14	17	31	12	11	16	6			
	2		1	10	4		1	9	1		6		3	2	8	1		4	2	1			
1	2	1	1	1	7	2	15	2	6		1	1											

Promotion/Relegation Play-Off

Snelders	McKimmie	Winnie	Grant	Irvine	Wright	Jess	Shearer	Kane	Dodds	Robertson	Hetherston	Booth	Miller	Woodthorpe	McKinnon	Smith	Watt	Glass	Inglis	Thomson	Aitken	Kpedekpo	
1	2		4	5	3		8		7				9			6			11	10			1st leg
1	2		4	5*	3		8	14	10				7			9†			6	11	12		2nd leg

61

1995-96

1	Aug	26	(a)	Falkirk	W	3-2	Inglis, Dodds, Booth	6,647
2	Sep	10	(h)	Celtic	L	2-3	Boyd (og), Jess	16,489
3		16	(a)	Hibernian	D	1-1	Shearer	11,161
4		23	(a)	Kilmarnock	W	2-1	Miller, Woodthorpe	7,198
5		30	(h)	Raith R	W	3-0	Booth 2, Miller	13,983
6	Oct	4	(a)	Hearts	W	2-1	Dodds, Booth	10,927
7		7	(h)	Rangers	L	0-1		20,351
8		14	(a)	Motherwell	L	1-2	Booth	6,842
9		21	(h)	Partick Thistle	W	3-0	Craig (og), Jess, Bernard	12,719
10		28	(a)	Celtic	L	0-2		32,275
11	Nov	4	(h)	Hibernian	L	1-2	Glass	14,774
12		8	(h)	Falkirk	W	3-1	Dodds, Miller, McGowan (og)	11,214
13		11	(a)	Rangers	D	1-1	Jess	45,427
14		18	(a)	Raith R	L	0-1		5,786
15	Dec	22	(a)	Partick Thistle	L	0-1		4,286
16		9	(h)	Motherwell	W	1-0	Shearer	11,299
17		13	(h)	Kilmarnock	W	4-1	Miller 3, Windass	14,060
18		16	(h)	Hearts	L	1-2	Windass	12,308
19	Jan	8	(a)	Hibernian	W	2-1	Miller, Dodds	8,191
20		14	(h)	Celtic	L	1-2	Dodds	16,760
21		16	(a)	Falkirk	D	1-1	Windass	4,003
22		20	(h)	Partick Thistle	W	1-0	Dodds	9,149
23		23	(a)	Kilmarnock	D	1-1	Irvine	6,703
24	Feb	7	(h)	Raith R	W	1-0	Windass	6,628
25		10	(a)	Hearts	W	3-1	Windass, Shearer, Glass	14,314
26		13	(a)	Motherwell	L	0-1		5,090
27		25	(h)	Rangers	L	0-1		19,842
28	Mar	2	(h)	Kilmarnock	W	3-0	Booth 2, Miller	7,177
29		16	(a)	Raith R	D	2-2	Miller, Buchan	4,932
30		23	(h)	Hibernian	W	2-1	Dodds, Booth	10,924
31	Apr	1	(a)	Celtic	L	0-5		35,284
32		13	(h)	Motherwell	W	2-1	McCart (og), Irvine	8,943
33		16	(a)	Partick Thistle	D	1-1	Booth	4,568
34		20	(h)	Hearts	D	1-1	Windass	11,303
35		28	(a)	Rangers	L	1-3	Irvine	47,247
36	May	4	(h)	Falkirk	W	2-1	Glass, McGowan (og)	11,831

FINAL LEAGUE POSITION: 3rd in Premier Division

Appearances

Sub. Appearances

Goals

62

Snelders	McKimmie	Woodthorpe	Hetherston	Inglis	Smith	Miller	Jess	Booth	Dodds	Glass	Thomson	Shearer	McKinnon	Watt	Christie	Bernard	Grant	Robertson	Windass	Irvine	Buchan	Rowson	Kpedekope	Craig	
1	2	3	4	5	6	7*	8	9	10	11	12														1
1	2	3	4†	5	6	7*	8	9	10	11		12	13												2
1	2	3	4	5	6	7	8	9*	10	11		12													3
	2	3	4	5	6	7*	8	9†	10	11		12		1	13										4
	2	3	4	5	6	7*	8	9	10†	11		13		1	12										5
	2	3	4	5	6	7*	8	9†	10	11		13		1	12										6
	2	3	4†	5	6	7	8	9	10*	11		12		1											7
	2	3†	4	5	6	7	8	9*	10	11		12		1											8
	2*			5	6	7	11		10	3	12	8		1		9	4								9
15	2	13		5	6	7*	11	9	10	3†		12		1°		8	4								10
1	2			5	6	7	11	9*	10	3		12				8	4								11
1	2		13	5	6	7	11		10†	3*	12	8				9	4								12
1	2			5	6	7	11	9	10*	3		12				8	4								13
	2		11†	5	6	7		9	10*	3		12		1		8	4								14
	2			5	6	7†	11*		10		13	8		1		9	4	3	12						15
					6	7	11		10	3		8		1		4	2	9	5						16
	2				6	7†	11		10*	3		8		1		4	12	9	5						17
					6	7	11		10*	3		8		1		4	2	12	9	5					18
	2			5	6	7	11		10	3				1		9	4		8						19
	2			5	6	7*	11		10	3		12		1		9	4		8						20
	2			5	6	7	11*		10	3†		12		1		9	4		8						21
	2			5*	6	7	11		10†	3		13		1		9	4		8		12				22
	2				6	7	11			3		10		1	12	9	4*		8	5					23
	2				6	7	11	12		3		8*		1		9	4		10	5					24
	2				6	7	11*	12		3		8		1		9	4		10	5					25
	2				6	7	11*			3	12	8		1		9	4		10	5					26
	2*				6	7		12	10	3		8		1		11	4		9	5					27
		3			6	7*		9	10	11†				1		4	2	8		5	12	13			28
		3			6	7		9	12			8*		1		2	11†	10		5		13	4		29
		3			6	7		9†	12			8*		1	10	2	11			5		13	4		30
		3			6	7		9†	10	11*				1		4	2	12	8	5		13			31
	2	3			6		13		10°	11*		8†		1		7	12	9		5			4	14	32
	2	3			6			9*	10			12		1		7	11†		8	5		4	13		33
	2	3*			6			9†		11		8		1		7	12	10		5		13	4		34
	2				6	3		9	10	11				1		7*			8	5		12	4		35
					6	4		9†		11				1		7*	12		8	5	2	3	10	13	36
6	29	15	9	24	33	31	25	20	28	32		15		30		27	22	5	19	17	1	7	1		
1		2				4	3		4	15	1			2		4	3	6	1	1	3	2	4	1	
		1	1		9	3	9	7	3		3			1					6	3	1				

63

CUP COMPETITIONS – 1971/72 TO 1995/96

SCOTTISH F.A. CUP
1971/72 SEASON
3rd Round
Feb 5 vs Dundee United (a) 4-0
Att: 12,974 R. Miller, Harper 2 (1 pen), Young
4th Round
Feb 26 vs Morton (h) 1-0
Att: 18,277 Willoughby
5th Round
Mar 18 vs Hibernian (a) 0-2
Att: 25,936

1972/73 SEASON
3rd Round
Feb 3 vs Brechin City (a) 4-2
Att: 8,123 Mitchell 2, Jarvie, Own Goal
4th Round
Feb 28 vs Falkirk (h) 3-1
Att: 17,730 Forrest, Purdie, S. Murray
5th Round
Mar 17 vs Celtic (a) 0-0
Att: 40,032
Replay
Mar 21 vs Celtic (h) 0-1
Att: 33,465

1973/74 SEASON
3rd Round
Jan 27 vs Dundee (h) 0-2
Att: 23,574

1974/75 SEASON
3rd Round
Jan 25 vs Rangers (h) 1-1
Att: 30,000 W. Miller
Replay
Feb 10 vs Rangers (a) 2-1 (aet.)
Att: 52,000 Graham, Davidson
4th Round
Feb 19 vs Dundee United (a) 1-0
Att: 22,000 Jarvie
5th Round
Mar 8 vs Motherwell (h) 0-1
Att: 23,400

1975/76 SEASON
3rd Round
Jan 24 vs Alloa Athletic (a) 4-0
Att: 6,312 Scott, McMaster, Miller, Robb
4th Round
Feb 14 vs Rangers (a) 1-4
Att: 52,000 Smith

1976/77 SEASON
3rd Round
Jan 29 vs Dunfermline Athletic (a) 1-0
Att: 11,899 Harper
4th Round
Feb 26 vs Dundee (a) 0-0
Att: 16,999
Replay
Mar 2 vs Dundee (h) 1-2
Att: 18,375 Davidson

1977/78 SEASON
3rd Round
Feb 6 vs Ayr United (h) 2-0
Att: 14,244 Harper 2 (1 pen)
4th Round
Feb 27 vs St. Johnstone (h) 3-0
Att: 15,597 Davidson, Harper, Jarvie

5th Round
Mar 11 vs Morton (h) 2-2
Att: 17,394 Davidson, Jarvie
Replay
Mar 15 vs Morton (a) 2-1
Att: 10,500 McMaster (pen), Fleming
Semi-Final (at Hampden Park)
Apr 12 vs Partick Thistle 4-2
Att: 12,282 Fleming 3, Harper (pen)
FINAL (at Hampden Park)
May 6 vs Rangers 1-2
Att: 61,563 Ritchie

1978/79 SEASON
3rd Round
Jan 27 vs Hamilton Academical (a) 2-0
Att: 9,400 Miller, Harper
4th Round
Feb 21 vs Ayr United (h) 6-2
Att: 11,500 Archibald 2, McMaster, Scanlon 2, Harper
5th Round
Mar 10 vs Celtic (h) 1-1
Att: 23,000 Harper
Replay
Mar 14 vs Celtic (a) 2-1
Att: 36,000 Davidson, Archibald
Semi-Final (at Hampden Park)
Apr 11 vs Hibernian 1-2
Att: 9,837 Archibald

1979/80 SEASON
3rd Round
Jan 26 vs Arbroath (a) 1-1
Att: 5,764 Archibald
Replay
Jan 30 vs Arbroath (h) 5-0
Att: 9,127 Hamilton, Scanlon 3 (1 pen), Archibald
4th Round
Feb 16 vs Airdrieonians (h) 8-0
Att: 10,410 Archibald 4, Miller, Strachan, McMaster, Scanlon
5th Round
Mar 8 vs Partick Thistle (a) 2-1
Att: 8,584 Jarvie, Archibald
Semi-Final (at Parkhead)
Apr 12 vs Rangers 0-1
Att: 44,000

1980/81 SEASON
3rd Round
Jan 24 vs Raith Rovers (a) 2-1
Att: 10,000 Jarvie, McGhee
4th Round
Feb 14 vs Morton (a) 0-1
Att: 8,350

1981/82 SEASON
3rd Round
Jan 23 vs Motherwell (a) 1-0
Att: 12,679 Hewitt
4th Round
Feb 13 vs Celtic (h) 1-0
Att: 24,000 Hewitt
5th Round
Mar 6 vs Kilmarnock (h) 4-2
Att: 12,000 McGhee, Simpson, Strachan 2 (2 pens)
Semi-Final (at Parkhead)
Apr 3 vs St. Mirren 1-1
Att: 16,782 Strachan (pen)

Replay (at Dens Park)
Apr 7 vs St. Mirren 3-2
Att: 15,663 McGhee, Simpson, Weir
FINAL (at Hampden Park)
May 22 vs Rangers 4-1 (aet.)
Att: 53,788 McLeigh, McGhee, Strachan, Cooper

1982/83 SEASON
3rd Round
Jan 29 vs Hibernian (a) 4-1
Att: 14,290 Weir, Simpson, Watson, McGhee
4th Round
Feb 19 vs Dundee (h) 1-0
Att: 19,000 Simpson
5th Round
Mar 12 vs Partick Thistle (a) 2-1
Att: 12,400 Cooper, Weir
Semi-Final (at Hampden Park)
Apr 16 vs Celtic 1-0
Att: 51,100 Weir
FINAL (at Hampden Park)
May 21 vs Rangers 1-0 (aet.)
Att: 62,979 Black

1983/84 SEASON
3rd Round
Feb 13 vs Kilmarnock (h) 1-1
Att: 15,000 Weir
Replay
Feb 15 vs Kilmarnock (a) 3-1
Att: 6,200 Strachan, Miller, Weir
4th Round
Feb 18 vs Clyde (a) 2-0
Att: 5,800 Angus, Cooper
5th Round
Mar 17 vs Dundee United (h) 0-0
Att: 20,000
Replay
Mar 28 vs Dundee United (a) 1-0
Att: 18,000 McGhee
Semi-Final (at Tynecastle)
Apr 14 vs Dundee 2-0
Att: 17,650 Porteous, Strachan
FINAL (at Hampden Park)
May 19 vs Celtic 2-1 (aet.)
Att: 58,900 Black, McGhee

1984/85 SEASON
3rd Round
Jan 30 vs Alloa Athletic (h) 5-0
Att: 13,500 Hewitt, Stark 3, Simpson
4th Round
Feb 16 vs Raith Rovers (a) 2-1
Att: 10,000 McDougall 2 (1 pen)
5th Round
Mar 9 vs Heart of Midlothian (a) 1-1
Att: 23,900 Black
Replay
Mar 13 vs Heart of Midlothian (h) 1-0
Att: 23,000 Stark
Semi-Final (at Tynecastle)
Apr 13 vs Dundee United 0-0
Att: 18,200
Replay (at Tynecastle)
Apr 17 vs Dundee United 1-2
Att: 10,771 Angus

1985/86 SEASON
3rd Round
Feb 4 vs Montrose (h) 4-1
Att: 9,000 Stark, W. Miller, McDougall, McLeish
4th Round
Feb 15 vs Arbroath (a) 1-0
Att: 6,000 J. Miller
5th Round
Mar 8 vs Dundee (a) 2-2
Att: 12,900 Hewitt 2
Replay
Mar 12 vs Dundee (h) 2-1 (aet.)
Att: 21,000 Black, Weir
Semi-Final (at Dens Park)
Apr 5 vs Hibernian 3-0
Att: 19,200 Stark, Black, J. Miller
FINAL (at Hampden Park)
May 10 vs Heart of Midlothian 3-0
Att: 62,841 Hewitt 2, Stark

1986/87 SEASON
3rd Round
Feb 1 vs Celtic (h) 2-2
Att: 23,000 Bett (pen), Hewitt
Replay
Feb 4 vs Celtic (a) 0-0 (aet.)
Att: 55,400
2nd Replay (at Dens Park)
Feb 9 vs Celtic 0-1
Att: 21,255

1987/88 SEASON
3rd Round
Jan 30 vs St. Johnstone (a) 1-0
Att: 10,000 Connor
4th Round
Feb 20 vs Hamilton Academical (a) 2-0
Att: 7,270 Nicholas C, Dodds
Quarter-Final
Mar 12 vs Clyde (h) 5-0
Att: 12,000 Dodds 3, Falconer, Edwards
Semi-Final (at Dens Park)
Apr 9 vs Dundee United 0-0
Att: 20,488
Replay (at Dens Park)
Apr 13 vs Dundee United 1-1 (aet.)
Att: 17,288 Nicholas C
2nd Replay (at Dens Park)
Apr 20 vs Dundee United 0-1
Att: 19,048

1988/89 SEASON
3rd Round
Jan 28 vs Dunfermline Athletic (a) 0-0
Att: 16,656
Replay
Feb 1 vs Dunfermline Athletic (h) 3-1
Att: 21,500 Wright 2, Nicholas
4th Round
Feb 18 vs Dundee (h) 1-1
Att: 23,000 Connor
Replay
Feb 22 vs Dundee (a) 1-1 (aet) (Full-time 0-0)
Att: 18,756 Grant
2nd Replay
Feb 27 vs Dundee (a) 0-1
Att: 21,095

1989/90 SEASON
3rd Round
Jan 20 vs Partick Thistle (a) 6-2
Att: 11,875 Van der Ark 3, Grant, Kerr (og), Mason

4th Round
Feb 24 vs Morton (h) 2-1
Att: 14,500 Gillhaus, Nicholas
Quarter-Final
Mar 17 vs Heart of Midlothian (h) 4-1
Att: 22,500 Bett, Gillhaus, Irvine, Nicholas
Semi-Final (at Tynecastle Park)
Apr 14 vs Dundee United 4-0
Att: 16,581 Irvine, Paatelainan (og), Van der Hoorn (og), Gillhaus
FINAL (at Hampden Park)
May 12 vs Celtic 0-0 (aet.)
Att: 60,493 Aberdeen won 9-8 on penalties

1990/91 SEASON
3rd Round
Jan 26 vs Motherwell (h) 0-1
Att: 15,000

1991/92 SEASON
3rd Round
Jan 22 vs Rangers (h) 0-1
Att: 23,000

1992/93 SEASON
3rd Round
Jan 9 vs Hamilton Academical (h) 4-1
Att: 10,800 Booth 3, Irvine
4th Round
Feb 7 vs Dundee United (h) 2-0
Att: 14,500 Jess 2
Quarter-Final
Mar 6 vs Clydebank (h) 1-1
Att: 11,300 Shearer (pen)
Replay
Mar 16 vs Clydebank (a) 4-3
Att: 8,000 Irvine, Paatelainen, Booth 2
Semi-Final (at Tynecastle Park)
Apr 3 vs Hibernian 1-0
Att: 21,414
FINAL (at Celtic Park)
May 29 vs Rangers 1-2
Att: 50,715 Richardson

1993/94 SEASON
3rd Round
Feb 8 vs East Stirling (a) 3-1
Att: 3,853 Craig (og), Shearer 2
4th Round
Feb 19 vs Raith Rovers (h) 1-0
Att: 13,740 Miller
Quarter-Final
Mar 12 vs St. Johnstone (a) 1-1
Att: 8,447 Booth
Replay
Mar 15 vs St. Johnstone (h) 2-0
Att: 14,325 Shearer, Richardson
Semi-Final (at Hampden Park)
Apr 9 vs Dundee United 1-1
Att: 21,397 Shearer
Replay (at Hampden Park)
Apr 12 vs Dundee United 0-1
Att: 13,936

1994/95 SEASON
3rd Round
Jan 28 vs Stranraer (h) 1-0
Att: 9,183 Jess
4th Round
Feb 18 vs Stenhousemuir (a) 0-2
Att: 3,452

1995/96 SEASON
3rd Round
Jan 30 vs Motherwell (a) 2-0
Att: 6,035 Windass, Shearer
4th Round
Feb 17 vs Stirling Albion (a) 2-0
Att: 3,808 Windass, Shearer
Quarter-Final
Mar 9 vs Airdrieonians (h) 2-1
Att: 11,749 Windass, Bernard
Semi-Final (at Hampden Park)
Apr 6 vs Heart of Midlothian 1-2
Att: 27,785 Shearer

SCOTTISH LEAGUE CUP

1971/72 SEASON
Preliminary Round, Game One
Aug 14 vs Dundee (h) 1-1
Att: 19,053 Robb
Preliminary Round, Game Two
Aug 18 vs Clyde (a) 2-0
Att: 2,027 Harper 2
Preliminary Round, Game Three
Aug 21 vs Falkirk (h) 1-0
Att: 17,339 Harper
Preliminary Round, Game Four
Aug 25 vs Clyde (h) 5-0
Att: 15,542 Graham 3, Harper, Willoughby
Preliminary Round, Game Five
Aug 28 vs Dundee (h) 1-3
Att: 11,875 Willoughby
Preliminary Round, Game Six
Sep 1 vs Falkirk (a) 1-3
Att: 11,865 Forrest

1972/73 SEASON
Preliminary Round, Game One
Aug 12 vs Queen of the South (a) 4-0
Att: 4,673 G. Buchan, Jarvie, Hermiston, Own Goal
Preliminary Round, Game Two
Aug 16 vs Hibernian (h) 4-1
Att: 20,998 Jarvie 2, Harper 2
Preliminary Round, Game Three
Aug 19 vs Queen's Park (h) 5-1
Att: 11,464 Young 2, Harper 2, Jarvie
Preliminary Round, Game Four
Jan 23 vs Hibernian (a) 1-2
Att: 17,133 Jarvie
Preliminary Round, Game Five
Aug 26 vs Queen of the South (h) 2-1
Att: 10,144 Taylor, Purdie
Preliminary Round, Game Six
Aug 30 vs Queen's Park (a) 3-0
Att: 1,029 Harper 3
2nd Round (1st leg)
Sep 20 vs Falkirk (h) 8-0
Att: 9,939 Forrest, Jarvie 2, Harper 3 (1 pen) Graham, Robb
2nd Round (2nd leg)
Oct 4 vs Falkirk (a) 2-3 (aggregate 10-3)
Att: 4,000 Harper 2
Quarter-Final (1st leg)
Oct 11 vs East Fife (h) 3-0
Att: 13,605 Taylor, Jarvie, Harper
Quarter-Final (2nd leg)
Nov 1 vs East Fife (a) 4-1 (aggregate 7-1)
Att: 4,492 Harper, Jarvie 2, Own Goal
Semi-Final (at Hampden Park)
Nov 27 vs Celtic 2-3
Att: 39,682 Harper, Robb

65

1973/74 SEASON
Preliminary Round, Game One
Aug 11 vs Motherwell (h) 3-1
Att: 10,722 Hermiston (pen), Smith, Graham
Preliminary Round, Game Two
Aug 15 vs Dundee United (a) 0-0
Att: 6,000
Preliminary Round, Game Three
Aug 18 vs East Fife (h) 1-1
Att: 8,188 Williamson
Preliminary Round, Game Four
Aug 22 vs Dundee United (h) 0-2
Att: 8,912
Preliminary Round, Game Five
Aug 25 vs East Fife (a) 2-0
Att: 4,153 R. Miller, Graham
Preliminary Round, Game Six
Aug 29 vs Motherwell (a) 0-0
Att: 9,808
2nd Round (1st leg)
Sep 12 vs Stirling Albion (h) 3-0
Att: 7,500 Graham, Jarvie 2
2nd Round (2nd leg)
Oct 10 vs Stirling Albion (a) 3-0 (agg. 6-0)
Att: 3,000 Jarvie 3
Quarter-Final (1st leg)
Oct 31 vs Celtic (a) 2-3
Att: 26,000 Jarvie 2
Quarter-Final (2nd leg)
Nov 21 vs Celtic (h) 0-0 (aggregate 2-3)
Att: 15,500

1974/75 SEASON
Preliminary Round, Game One
Aug 10 vs Heart of Midlothian (h) 0-1
Att: 11,000
Preliminary Round, Game Two
Aug 14 vs Morton (a) 1-3
Att: 2,000 Hermiston
Preliminary Round, Game Three
Aug 17 vs Dunfermline Athletic (a) 1-3
Att: 4,500 Jarvie
Preliminary Round, Game Four
Aug 21 vs Morton (h) 4-0
Att: 5,000 Purdie, Thomson, Jarvie, Young
Preliminary Round, Game Five
Aug 24 vs Dunfermline Athletic (h) 3-0
Att: 7,000 Jarvie, Williamson, Purdie
Preliminary Round, Game Six
Aug 28 vs Heart of Midlothian (a) 1-2
Att: 14,000 Hermiston (pen)

1975/76 SEASON
Preliminary Round, Game One
Aug 9 vs Celtic (a) 0-1
Att: 32,000
Preliminary Round, Game Two
Aug 13 vs Dumbarton (h) 2-0
Att: 6,000 Graham, Jarvie
Preliminary Round, Game Three
Aug 16 vs Heart of Midlothian (h) 1-2
Att: 8,400 Williamson
Preliminary Round, Game Four
Aug 20 vs Dumbarton (a) 1-0
Att: 2,400 Hair
Preliminary Round, Game Five
Aug 23 vs Heart of Midlothian (a) 0-1
Att: 11,000
Preliminary Round, Game Six
Aug 27 vs Celtic (h) 0-2
Att: 13,000

1976/77 SEASON
Preliminary Round, Game One
Aug 14 vs Kilmarnock (h) 2-0
Att: 10,866 Harper, Graham
Preliminary Round, Game Two
Aug 18 vs St. Mirren (a) 3-2
Att: 4,500 Fleming 2, Harper
Preliminary Round, Game Three
Aug 21 vs Ayr United (h) 1-0
Att: 9,695 Harper (pen)
Preliminary Round, Game Four
Aug 25 vs St. Mirren (h) 4-0
Att: 8,212 Harper 2 (1 pen), Williamson 2
Preliminary Round, Game Five
Aug 28 vs Ayr United (a) 1-1
Att: 4,800 Harper
Preliminary Round, Game Six
Sep 1 vs Kilmarnock (a) 1-2
Att: 2,700 Harper
Quarter-Final (1st leg)
Sep 22 vs Stirling Albion (h) 1-0
Att: 7,185 Harper
Quarter-Final (2nd leg)
Oct 6 vs Stirling Alb. (a) 0-1 (aet) (agg 1-1)
Att: 3,700
Replay (at Dens Park)
Oct 18 vs Stirling Albion 2-0
Att: 4,027 Scott, Smith
Semi-Final (at Hampden Park)
Oct 27 vs Rangers 5-1
Att: 20,990 Scott 3, Harper, Jarvie
FINAL (at Hampden Park)
Nov 6 vs Celtic 2-1
Att: 69,679 Jarvie, Robb

1977/78 SEASON
1st Round (1st leg)
Aug 17 vs Airdrieonians (h) 3-1
Att: 10,600 Fleming 2, Shirra
1st Round (2nd leg)
Aug 24 vs Airdrieonians (a) 2-0 (agg. 5-1)
Att: 7,000 McMaster 2
2nd Round (1st leg)
Aug 31 vs Cowdenbeath (h) 5-0
Att: 8,250 Harper 3, Fleming 2
2nd Round (2nd leg)
Sep 3 vs Cowdenbeath (a) 5-0 (agg. 10-0)
Att: 1,780 Davidson, McMaster, Harper 3 (1 pen)
3rd Round (1st leg)
Oct 5 vs Rangers (a) 1-6
Att: 25,000 Davidson
3rd Round (2nd leg)
Oct 26 vs Rangers (h) 3-1 (aggregate 4-7)
Att: 15,600 Smith, Jarvie 2

1978/79 SEASON
2nd Round (1st leg)
Aug 30 vs Meadowbank Thistle (a) 5-0
Att: 1,600 Sullivan, Jarvie, Kennedy, Archibald, Fleming
2nd Round (2nd leg)
Sep 2 vs Meadowbank T. (h) 4-0 (agg. 9-0)
Att: 6,850 Archibald, Harper 2, Scanlon
3rd Round (1st leg)
Oct 4 vs Hamilton Academical (a) 1-0
Att: 5,000 Scanlon
3rd Round (2nd leg)
Oct 11 vs Hamilton Acad. (h) 7-1 (agg 8-1)
Att: 10,000 Rougvie, Harper 4 (2 pens), Sullivan, Kennedy

Quarter-Final (1st leg)
Nov 8 vs Ayr United (a) 3-3
Att: 6,300 Sullivan, Harper 2
Quarter-Final (2nd leg)
Nov 15 vs Ayr United (h) 3-1 (aggreg. 6-4)
Att: 13,000 McLelland, Harper, Archibald
Semi-Final (at Dens Park)
Dec 13 vs Hibernian 1-0 (aet.)
Att: 21,000 Kennedy
FINAL (at Hampden Park)
Mar 31 vs Rangers 1-2
Att: 54,000 Davidson

1979/80 SEASON
1st Round (1st leg)
Aug 15 vs Arbroath (h) 4-0
Att: 6,700 McGhee, Davidson, McMaster, Jarvie
1st Round (2nd leg)
Aug 22 vs Arbroath (a) 1-2 (aggregate 5-2)
Att: 2,174 Harper
2nd Round (1st leg)
Aug 29 vs Meadowbank Thistle (a) 5-0
Att: 1,200 McGhee, Strachan, McMaster 2, Garner
2nd Round (2nd leg)
Sep 1 vs Meadowbank Th. (h) 2-2 (agg 7-2)
Att: 6,000 McMaster, Strachan (pen)
3rd Round (1st leg)
Sep 26 vs Rangers (h) 3-1
Att: 18,000 Garner, Harper, McLeish
3rd Round (2nd leg)
Oct 10 vs Rangers (a) 2-0 (aggregate 5-1)
Att: 35,000 Harper, Strachan
Quarter-Final (1st leg)
Oct 31 vs Celtic (h) 3-2
Att: 24,000 Archibald 3
Quarter-Final (2nd leg)
Nov 24 vs Celtic (a) 1-0 (aggregate 4-2)
Att: 39,000 McGhee
Semi-Final (at Hampden Park)
Dec 1 vs Morton 2-1
Att: 11,900 McGhee, Strachan (pen)
FINAL (at Hampden Park)
Dec 8 vs Dundee United 0-0 (aet.)
Att: 27,173
FINAL REPLAY (at Dens Park)
Dec 12 vs Dundee United 0-3
Att: 29,000

1980/81 SEASON
2nd Round (1st leg)
Aug 27 vs Berwick Rangers (h) 8-1
Att: 7,570 McGhee 3, Jarvie 2, Watson 2, Bell
2nd Round (2nd leg)
Aug 30 vs Berwick Rang. (a) 4-0 (agg 12-1)
Att: 1,188 Strachan, Hewitt, De Clerck, Kennedy
3rd Round (1st leg)
Sep 3 vs Rangers (a) 0-1
Att: 30,000
3rd Round (2nd leg)
Sep 24 vs Rangers (h) 3-1 (aggregate 3-2)
Att: 23,926 McMaster, Strachan 2 (2 pens)
Quarter-Final (1st leg)
Oct 8 vs Dundee (a) 0-0
Att: 10,500
Quarter-Final (2nd leg)
Oct 29 vs Dundee (h) 0-1 (aggregate 0-1)
Att: 13,000

66

1981/82 SEASON

Preliminary Round, Game One
Aug 8 vs Kilmarnock (h) 3-0
Att: 9,000 McGhee 2, Kennedy

Preliminary Round, Game Two
Aug 12 vs Heart of Midlothian (a) 0-1
Att: 10,500

Preliminary Round, Game Three
Aug 15 vs Airdrieonians (h) 3-0
Att: 7,000 Hewitt, Weir, Strachan (pen)

Preliminary Round, Game Four
Aug 19 vs Heart of Midlothian (h) 3-0
Att: 8,600 Bell, Strachan (pen), Hewitt

Preliminary Round, Game Five
Aug 22 vs Kilmarnock (a) 3-0
Att: 3,100 Strachan 2 (1 pen), McGhee

Preliminary Round, Game Six
Aug 26 vs Airdrieonians (a) 0-0
Att: 3,000

Quarter-Final (1st leg)
Sep 2 vs Berwick Rangers (h) 5-0
Att: 6,500 Cooper, Strachan 2 (1 pen), Bell, McCall

Quarter-Final (2nd leg)
Sep 23 vs Berwick Rang. (a) 3-0 (agg. 8-0)
Att: 1,200 McMaster, McGhee, Harrow

Semi-Final (1st leg)
Oct 7 vs Dundee United (a) 1-0
Att: 15,000 Weir

Semi-Final (2nd leg)
Oct 28 vs Dundee United (h) 0-3 (agg. 1-3)
Att: 21,000

1982/83 SEASON

Preliminary Round, Game One
Aug 11 vs Morton (a) 2-2
Att: 3,500 Strachan (pen), McGhee

Preliminary Round, Game Two
Aug 14 vs Dundee (h) 3-3
Att: 9,000 Black 3

Preliminary Round, Game Three
Aug 21 vs Dumbarton (h) 3-0
Att: 6,500 McGhee, Strachan 2

Preliminary Round, Game Four
Aug 25 vs Morton (h) 3-0
Att: 11,000 Rougvie, Bell 2

Preliminary Round, Game Five
Aug 28 vs Dundee (a) 5-1
Att: 7,000 Strachan 4, McGhee

Preliminary Round, Game Six
Sep 8 vs Dumbarton (a) 2-1
Att: 2,500 Bell, Hewitt

Quarter-Final (1st leg)
Sep 22 vs Dundee United (a) 1-3
Att: 14,000 McGhee

Quarter-Final (2nd leg)
Oct 6 vs Dundee United (h) 0-1 (agg. 1-4)
Att: 11,700

1983/84 SEASON

2nd Round (1st leg)
Aug 24 vs Raith Rovers (h) 9-0
Att: 9,500 Stark 3, Porteous, Black 4 (1 pen) Hewitt

2nd Round (2nd leg)
Aug 27 vs Raith Rovers (a) 3-0 (agg. 12-0)
Att: 3,000 Hewitt 2, Stark

3rd Round, Game One
Aug 31 vs Meadowbank Thistle (h) 4-0
Att: 10,000 McGhee 2, Stark, Black

3rd Round, Game Two
Sep 7 vs St. Johnstone (a) 1-0
Att: 5,100 Miller

3rd Round, Game Three
Oct 5 vs Dundee (h) 0-0
Att: 13,200

3rd Round, Game Four
Oct 26 vs St. Johnstone (h) 1-0
Att: 12,700 Simpson

3rd Round, Game Five
Nov 9 vs Meadowbank Thistle (a) 3-1
Att: 2,700 Porteous, Own Goal, Hewitt

3rd Round, Game Six
Nov 30 vs Dundee (a) 2-1
Att: 11,000 McGhee, Bell

Semi-Final (1st leg)
Feb 22 vs Celtic (h) 0-0
Att: 20,000

Semi-Final (2nd leg)
Mar 10 vs Celtic (a) 0-1 (aggregate 0-1)
Att: 41,200

1984/85 SEASON

2nd Round
Aug 22 vs Airdrieonians (a) 1-3
Att: 5,000 Stark

1985/86 SEASON

2nd Round
Aug 21 vs Ayr United (h) 5-0
Att: 12,400 Stark 2, McQueen (pen), McDougall 2

3rd Round
Aug 28 vs St. Johnstone (a) 2-0
Att: 5,100 Hewitt, McDougall

Quarter-Final
Sep 4 vs Heart of Midlothian (h) 1-0
Att: 13,100 Black

Semi-Final (1st leg)
Sep 25 vs Dundee United (a) 1-0
Att: 12,400 Black

Semi-Final (2nd leg)
Oct 9 vs Dundee United (h) 1-0 (agg. 2-0)
Att: 20,000 McDougall

FINAL (at Hampden Park)
Oct 27 vs Hibernian 3-0
Att: 40,061 Black 2, Stark

1986/87 SEASON

2nd Round
Aug 20 vs Alloa Athletic (h) 4-0
Att: 8,000 Hewitt 2, Connor, J. Miller

3rd Round
Aug 27 vs Clyde (h) 3-1
Att: 9,000 Stark 2, J. Miller (pen)

Quarter-Final
Sep 3 vs Celtic (h) 1-1 (aet.)
Att: 22,000 Connor
Celtic won 4-2 on penalties

1987/88 SEASON

2nd Round
Aug 19 vs Brechin City (h) 5-1
Att: 9,000 Miller J 3, Hewitt, Irvine

3rd Round
Aug 29 vs St. Johnstone (h) 3-0
Att: 10,800 Dodds 2, Bett

Quarter-Final
Sep 1 vs Celtic (h) 1-0
Att: 24,000 Bett

Semi-Final (at Tannadice Park)
Sep 23 vs Dundee 2-0
Att: 22,034 Connor, Irvine

FINAL (at Hampden Park)
Oct 25 vs Rangers 3-3 (aet.)
Att: 71,961 Bett (pen), Hewitt, Falconer
Rangers won 5-3 on penalties

1988/89 SEASON

2nd Round
Aug 17 vs Arbroath (h) 4-0
Att: 9,139 Bett, Hewitt, Miller 2

3rd Round
Aug 23 vs Morton (a) 2-1
Att: 3,131 Bett 2

Quarter-Final
Aug 31 vs Hibernian (a) 2-1
Att: – Grant, Nicholas

Semi-Final (at Dens Park)
Sep 20 vs Dundee United 2-0
Att: 18,491 Hewitt, Dodds

FINAL (at Hampden Park)
Oct 23 vs Rangers 2-3
Att: 72,122 Dodds 2

1989/90 SEASON

2nd Round (at Fir Park)
Aug 15 vs Albion Rovers (a) 2-0
Att: 2,384 Robertson, Van der Ark

3rd Round
Aug 23 vs Airdrieonians (h) 4-0
Att: 10,000 Mason 2, Cameron, Bett

Quarter-Final
Aug 30 vs St. Mirren (h) 3-1
Att: 11,500 Mason, Bett, Winnie (og)

Semi-Final (at Hampden Park)
Sep 20 vs Celtic 1-0
Att: 45,367 Cameron

FINAL (at Hampden Park)
Oct 22 vs Rangers 2-1 (aet.)
Att: 61,190 Mason 2

1990/91 SEASON

2nd Round
Aug 21 vs Queen's Park (a) 2-1
Att: 2,201 Jess, Bett

3rd Round
Aug 29 vs Stranraer (h) 4-0
Att: 10,000 Mason 2. Van de Ven, Irvine

Quarter-Final
Sep 5 vs Heart of Midlothian (h) 3-0
Att: 15,500 Van de Ven, Mason, Bett (pen)

Semi-Final (at Hampden Park)
Sep 26 vs Rangers 0-1
Att: 40,855

1991/92 SEASON

2nd Round
Aug 21 vs Clyde (a) 4-0
Att: 2,107 Grant, Van de Ven, Winnie, Booth

3rd Round
Aug 28 vs Airdrieonians (h) 0-1
Att: 13,000

1992/93 SEASON

2nd Round
Aug 12 vs Arbroath (a) 4-0
Att: 4,130 Paatelainen 2, Shearer, Jess

3rd Round
Aug 19 vs Dunfermline Athletic (h) 1-0 (aet)
Att: 10,791 Paatelainen

Quarter-Final
Aug 26 vs Falkirk (a) 4-1
Att: 8,022 Shearer 3, Irvine

Semi-Final (at Hampden Park)
Sep 23 vs Celtic 1-0
Att: 40,618 Jess

FINAL (at Hampden Park)
Oct 25 vs Rangers 1-2 (aet.)
Att: 45,298 Shearer

1993/94 SEASON
2nd Round
Aug 10 vs Clydebank (h) 5-0
Att: 11,394 Shearer 3 (1 pen), McLeish, Richardson
3rd Round
Aug 24 vs Motherwell (h) 5-2
Att: 12,993 Shearer, Miller, Booth 2, Jess
Quarter-Final
Sep 1 vs Rangers (a) 1-2 (aet.)
Att: 44,928 Miller

1994/95 SEASON
2nd Round
Aug 17 vs Stranraer (h) 1-0
Att: 8,158 Shearer
3rd Round
Aug 30 vs Partick Thistle (a) 5-0
Att: 5,046 Shearer 3 (1 pen), Kane, Dodds
Quarter-Final
Sep 21 vs Falkirk (a) 4-1
Att: 9,450 Booth 3, Rice (og)
Semi-Final (at Ibrox Stadium)
Oct 26 vs Celtic 0-1
Att: 44,000

1995/96 SEASON
2nd Round
Aug 19 vs St. Mirren (h) 3-1
Att: 10,397 Dodds, Booth 2
3rd Round
Aug 30 vs Falkirk (a) 4-1
Att: 6,387 Booth, Clark (og), Woodthorpe, Miller
Quarter-Final
Sep 20 vs Motherwell (a) 2-1 (aet.)
Att: 9,137 Dodds, Inglis
Semi-Final (at Hampden Park)
Oct 24 vs Rangers 2-1
Att: 26,131 Dodds 2
FINAL (at Hampden Park)
Nov 26 vs Dundee 2-0
Att: 33,096 Dodds, Shearer

EUROPEAN CUP
1980/81 SEASON
1st Round (1st leg)
Sep 17 vs Austria Vienna (h) 1-0
Att: 20,000 McGhee
1st Round (2nd leg)
Oct 1 vs Austria Vienna (a) 0-0 (agg. 1-0)
Att: 35,000
2nd Round (1st leg)
Oct 22 vs Liverpool (h) 0-1
Att: 24,000
2nd Round (2nd leg)
Nov 5 vs Liverpool (a) 0-4 (aggregate 0-5)
Att: 36,182

1984/85 SEASON
1st Round (1st leg)
Sep 19 vs Dynamo Berlin (h) 2-1
Att: 21,500 Black 2
1st Round (2nd leg)
Oct 3 vs Dyn. Berlin (a) 1-2 (aet) (agg. 3-3)
Att: 26,000 Angus
Dynamo Berlin won 5-4 on penalties

1985/86 SEASON
1st Round (1st leg)
Sep 18 vs Akranes (a) 3-1
Att: 7,000 Black, Hewitt, Stark

1st Round (2nd leg)
Oct 2 vs Akranes (h) 4-1 (aggregate 7-2)
Att: 14,500 Simpson, Hewitt, Gray, Falconer
2nd Round (1st leg)
Oct 23 vs Servette (a) 0-0
Att: 7,500
2nd Round (2nd leg)
Nov 6 vs Servette (h) 1-0 (aggregate 1-0)
Att: 19,000 McDougall
Quarter-Final (1st leg)
Mar 5 vs IFK Gothenburg (h) 2-2
Att: 22,000 W. Miller, Hewitt
Quarter-Final (2nd leg)
Mar 19 vs IFK Gothenburg (a) 0-0 (agg 2-2)
Att: 44,152
IFK Gothenburg won on the Away Goals rule

EUROPEAN CUP-WINNERS CUP
1978/79 SEASON
1st Round (1st leg)
Sep 13 vs Marek Stanke (a) 2-3
Att: 20,000 Jarvie, Harper
1st Round (2nd leg)
Sep 27 vs Marek Stanke (h) 3-0 (agg. 5-3)
Att: 25,000 Strachan, Jarvie, Harper
2nd Round (1st leg)
Oct 18 vs Fortuna Dusseldorf (a) 0-3
Att: 10,500
2nd Round (2nd leg)
Nov 1 vs Fort. Dusseldorf (h) 2-0 (agg. 2-3)
Att: 16,800 McLelland, Jarvie

1982/83 SEASON
Preliminary Round (1st leg)
Aug 18 vs Sion (h) 7-0
Att: 12,013 Black 2, Strachan, Hewitt, Simpson, McGhee, Kennedy
Preliminary Round (2nd leg)
Sep 1 vs Sion (a) 4-1 (aggregate 11-1)
Att: 2,400 Hewitt, Miller, McGhee 2
1st Round (1st leg)
Sep 15 vs Dinamo Tirana (h) 1-0
Att: 14,500 Hewitt
1st Round (2nd leg)
Sep 29 vs Dinamo Tirana (a) 0-0 (agg. 1-0)
Att: 25,000
2nd Round (1st leg)
Oct 20 vs Lech Poznan (h) 2-0
Att: 17,425 McGhee, Weir
2nd Round (2nd leg)
Nov 3 vs Lech Poznan (a) 1-0 (aggreg. 3-0)
Att: 33,000 Bell
Quarter-Final (1st leg)
Mar 2 vs Bayern Munich (a) 0-0
Att: 25,000
Quarter-Final (2nd leg)
Mar 16 vs Bayern Munich (h) 3-2 (agg 3-2)
Att: 24,000 Simpson, McLeish, Hewitt
Semi-Final (1st leg)
Apr 6 vs Waterschei (h) 5-1
Att: 24,000 Black, Simpson, McGhee 2, Weir
Semi-Final (2nd leg)
Apr 19 vs Waterschei (a) 0-1 (aggreg. 5-2)
Att: 20,000
FINAL (in Gothenburg)
May 11 vs Real Madrid 2-1 (aet.)
Att: 17,804 Black, Hewitt

1983/84 SEASON
1st Round (1st leg)
Sep 14 vs Akranes (a) 2-1
Att: 5,400 McGhee 2
1st Round (2nd leg)
Sep 28 vs Akranes (h) 1-1 (aggregate 3-2)
Att: 8,000 Strachan (pen)
2nd Round (1st leg)
Oct 19 vs Beveren (a) 0-0
Att: 15,000
2nd Round (2nd leg)
Nov 2 vs Beveren (h) 4-0 (aggregate 4-0)
Att: 24,000 Strachan 2 (1 pen), Simpson, Weir
Quarter-Final (1st leg)
Mar 7 vs Ujpest Doza (a) 0-2
Att: 25,000
Quarter-Final (2nd leg)
Mar 21 vs Ujpest Doza (h) 3-0 (agg. 3-2)
Att: 22,800 McGhee 3
Semi-Final (1st leg)
Apr 11 vs FC Porto (a) 0-1
Att: 70,000
Semi-Final (2nd leg)
Apr 25 vs FC Porto (h) 0-1 (aggregate 0-2)
Att: 23,000

1986/87 SEASON
1st Round (1st leg)
Sep 17 vs Sion (h) 2-1
Att: 12,500 Bett (pen), Wright
1st Round (2nd leg)
Oct 1 vs Sion (a) 0-3 (aggregate 2-4)
Att: 11,800

1990/91 SEASON
1st Round (1st leg)
Sep 19 vs Famagusta (a) 2-0
Att: 7,000 Mason, Gillhaus
1st Round (2nd leg)
Oct 3 vs Famagusta (h) 3-0 (aggregate 5-0)
Att: 7,000 Robertson C, Andreou A (og), Jess
2nd Round (1st leg)
Oct 24 vs Legia Warsaw (h) 0-0
Att: 16,000
2nd Round (2nd leg)
Nov 7 vs Legia Warsaw (a) 0-1 (agg. 0-1)
Att: 5,665

1993/94 SEASON
1st Round (1st leg)
Sep 14 vs Valur (a) 3-0
Att: 656 Shearer, Jess 2
1st Round (2nd leg)
Sep 29 vs Valur (h) 4-0 (aggregate 7-0)
Att: 10,000 Miller, Jess 2, Irvine
2nd Round (1st leg)
Oct 20 vs Torino (a) 2-3
Att: 30,000 Paatelainen, Jess
2nd Round (2nd leg)
Nov 3 vs Torino (h) 1-2 (aggregate 3-5)
Att: 21,655 Richardson

UEFA CUP
1971/72 SEASON
1st Round (1st leg)
Sep 15 vs Celta Vigo (a) 2-0
Att: 35,000 Harper, Own Goal
1st Round (2nd leg)
Sep 29 vs Celta Vigo (h) 1-0 (aggreg. 3-0)
Att: 30,000 Harper

2nd Round (1st leg)
Oct 27 vs Juventus (a) 0-2
Att: 35,000

2nd Round (2nd leg)
Nov 17 vs Juventus (h) 1-1 (aggregate 1-3)
Att: 29,500 Harper

1972/73 SEASON
1st Round (1st leg)
Sep 13 vs Borus. Moenchengladbach (h) 2-3
Att: 23,000 Harper, Jarvie

1st Round (2nd leg)
Sep 27 vs Borussia Moenc. (a) 3-6 (agg 5-9)
Att: 25,000 Harper 2, Jarvie

1973/74 SEASON
1st Round (1st leg)
Sep 19 vs Finn Harps (h) 4-1
Att: 10,700 R. Miller, Jarvie 2, Graham

1st Round (2nd leg)
Oct 3 vs Finn Harps (a) 3-1 (aggregate 7-2)
Att: 5,000 Robb, Graham, R. Miller

2nd Round (1st leg)
Oct 24 vs Tottenham Hotspur (h) 1-1
Att: 30,000 Hermiston (pen)

2nd Round (2nd leg)
Nov 7 vs Tott'ham Hotspur (a) 1-4 (agg 2-5)
Att: 21,785 Jarvie

1974/75 SEASON
1st Round (1st leg)
Sep 14 vs RWD Molenbeek (a) 0-0
Att: 14,000

1st Round (2nd leg)
Sep 28 vs RWD Molenbeek (h) 1-2 (agg 1-2)
Att: 20,000 Jarvie

1979/80 SEASON
1st Round (1st leg)
Sep 19 vs Eintracht Frankfurt (h) 1-1
Att: 18,000 Harper

1st Round (2nd leg)
Oct 3 vs Eintracht Frankfurt (a) 0-1 (agg 1-2)
Att: 12,000

1981/82 SEASON
1st Round (1st leg)
Sep 16 vs Ipswich Town (a) 1-1
Att: 18,535 Hewitt

1st Round (2nd leg)
Sep 30 vs Ipswich Town (h) 3-1 (agg. 4-2)
Att: 24,000 Strachan, Weir 2

2nd Round (1st leg)
Oct 21 vs Arges Pitesti (h) 3-0
Att: 17,000 Strachan, Weir, Hewitt

2nd Round (2nd leg)
Nov 4 vs Arges Pitesti (a) 2-2 (aggreg. 5-2)
Att: 15,000 Strachan (pen), Hewitt

3rd Round (1st leg)
Nov 25 vs Hamburg (h) 3-2
Att: 24,000 Black, Watson, Hewitt

3rd Round (2nd leg)
Dec 9 vs Hamburg (a) 1-3 (aggregate 4-5)
Att: 45,600 McGhee

1987/88 SEASON
1st Round (1st leg)
Sep 15 vs Bohemians Dublin (a) 0-0
Att: 10,000

1st Round (2nd leg)
Sep 30 vs Bohemians Dub. (h) 1-0 (agg 1-0)
Att: 10,000 Bett (pen)

2nd Round (1st leg)
Oct 21 vs Feyenoord (h) 2-1
Att: 16,000 Falconer, Miller J

2nd Round (2nd leg)
Nov 4 vs Feyenoord (a) 0-1 (aggregate 2-2)
Att: 22,000
Feyenoord won on the Away Goals rule

1988/89 SEASON
1st Round (1st leg)
Sep 7 vs Dynamo Dresden (h) 0-0
Att: 14,500

1st Round (2nd leg)
Oct 5 vs Dynamo Dresden (a) 0-2 (agg. 0-2)
Att: 36,000

1989/90 SEASON
1st Round (1st leg)
Sep 13 vs Rapid Vienna (h) 2-1
Att: 16,800 Robertson C, Grant

1st Round (2nd leg)
Sep 27 vs Rapid Vienna (a) 0-1 (agg. 2-2)
Att: 19,000
Rapid Vienna won on the Away Goals rule

1991/92 SEASON
1st Round (1st leg)
Sep 18 vs B 1903 Copenhagen (h) 0-1
Att: 13,000

1st Round (2nd leg)
Oct 2 vs B 1903 Copenh'n (a) 0-2 (agg 0-3)
Att: 5,237

1994/95 SEASON
Preliminary Round (1st leg)
Aug 9 vs Skonto Riga (a) 0-0
Att: 2,300

Preliminary Round (2nd leg)
Aug 23 vs Skonto Riga (h) 1-1 (aggreg. 1-1)
Att: 8,500 Kane
Skonto Riga won on the Away Goals rule

1971-72 SEASON
FIRST DIVISION

Celtic	34	28	4	2	96	28	60
Aberdeen	**34**	**21**	**8**	**5**	**80**	**26**	**50**
Rangers	34	21	2	11	71	38	44
Hibernian	34	19	6	9	62	34	44
Dundee	34	14	13	7	59	38	41
Heart of Midlothian	34	13	13	8	53	49	39
Partick Thistle	34	12	10	12	53	54	34
St. Johnstone	34	12	8	14	52	58	32
Dundee United	34	12	7	15	55	70	31
Motherwell	34	11	7	16	49	69	29
Kilmarnock	34	11	6	17	49	64	28
Ayr United	34	9	10	15	40	58	28
Morton	34	10	7	17	46	52	27
Falkirk	34	10	7	17	44	60	27
Airdrieonians	34	7	12	15	44	76	26
East Fife	34	5	15	14	34	61	25
Clyde	34	7	10	17	33	66	24
Dunfermline Athletic	34	7	9	18	31	50	23

1972-73 SEASON
FIRST DIVISION

Celtic	34	26	5	3	93	28	57
Rangers	34	26	4	4	74	30	56
Hibernian	34	19	7	8	74	33	45
Aberdeen	**34**	**16**	**11**	**7**	**61**	**34**	**43**
Dundee	34	17	9	8	68	43	43
Ayr United	34	16	8	10	50	51	40
Dundee United	34	17	5	12	56	51	39
Motherwell	34	11	9	14	38	48	31
East Fife	34	11	8	15	46	54	30
Heart of Midlothian	34	12	6	16	39	50	30
St. Johnstone	34	10	9	15	52	67	29
Morton	34	10	8	16	47	53	28
Partick Thistle	34	10	8	16	40	53	28
Falkirk	34	7	12	15	38	56	26
Arbroath	34	9	8	17	39	63	26
Dumbarton	34	6	11	17	43	72	23
Kilmarnock	34	7	8	19	40	71	22
Airdrieonians	34	4	8	22	34	75	16

1973-74 SEASON
FIRST DIVISION

Celtic	34	23	7	4	82	27	53
Hibernian	34	20	9	5	75	42	49
Rangers	34	21	6	7	67	34	48
Aberdeen	**34**	**13**	**16**	**5**	**46**	**26**	**42**
Dundee	34	16	7	11	67	48	39
Heart of Midlothian	34	14	10	10	54	43	38
Ayr United	34	15	8	11	44	40	38
Dundee United	34	15	7	12	55	51	37
Motherwell	34	14	7	13	45	40	35
Dumbarton	34	11	7	16	43	58	29
Partick Thistle	34	9	10	15	33	46	28
St. Johnstone	34	9	10	15	41	60	28
Arbroath	34	10	7	17	52	69	27
Morton	34	8	10	16	37	49	26
Clyde	34	8	9	17	29	65	25
Dunfermline Athletic	34	8	8	18	43	65	24
East Fife	34	9	6	19	26	51	24
Falkirk	34	4	14	16	33	58	22

1974-75 SEASON
FIRST DIVISION

Rangers	34	25	6	3	86	33	56
Hibernian	34	20	9	5	69	37	49
Celtic	34	20	5	9	81	41	45
Dundee United	34	19	7	8	72	43	45
Aberdeen	**34**	**16**	**9**	**9**	**66**	**43**	**41**
Dundee	34	16	6	12	48	42	38
Ayr United	34	14	8	11	50	61	36
Heart of Midlothian	34	11	13	10	47	52	35
St. Johnstone	34	11	12	11	41	44	34
Motherwell	34	14	5	15	52	57	33
Airdrieonians	34	11	9	14	43	55	31
Kilmarnock	34	8	15	11	52	68	31
Partick Thistle	34	10	10	14	48	62	30
Dumbarton	34	7	10	17	44	55	24
Dunfermline Athletic	34	7	9	18	46	66	23
Clyde	34	6	10	18	40	63	22
Morton	34	6	10	18	31	62	22
Arbroath	34	5	7	22	34	66	17

1975-76 SEASON
PREMIER DIVISION

Rangers	36	23	8	5	59	24	54
Celtic	36	21	6	9	71	42	48
Hibernian	36	20	7	9	58	40	43
Motherwell	36	16	8	12	57	49	40
Heart of Midlothian	36	13	9	14	39	44	35
Ayr United	36	14	5	17	46	59	33
Aberdeen	**36**	**11**	**10**	**15**	**49**	**50**	**32**
Dundee United	36	12	8	16	46	48	32
Dundee	36	11	10	15	49	62	32
St. Johnstone	36	3	5	28	29	79	11

1976-77 SEASON
PREMIER DIVISION

Celtic	36	23	9	4	79	39	55
Rangers	36	18	10	8	62	37	46
Aberdeen	**36**	**16**	**11**	**9**	**56**	**42**	**43**
Dundee United	36	16	9	11	54	45	41
Partick Thistle	36	11	13	12	40	44	35
Hibernian	36	8	18	10	34	35	34
Motherwell	36	10	12	14	57	60	32
Ayr United	36	11	8	17	44	68	30
Heart of Midlothian	36	7	13	16	49	66	27
Kilmarnock	36	4	9	23	32	71	17

70

1977-78 SEASON

PREMIER DIVISION

Rangers	36	24	7	5	76	39	55
Aberdeen	**36**	**22**	**9**	**5**	**68**	**29**	**53**
Dundee United	36	16	8	12	42	32	40
Hibernian	36	15	7	14	51	43	37
Celtic	36	15	6	15	63	54	36
Motherwell	36	13	7	16	45	52	33
Partick Thistle	36	14	5	17	52	64	33
St. Mirren	36	11	8	17	52	63	30
Ayr United	36	9	6	21	36	68	24
Clydebank	36	6	7	23	23	64	19

1978-79 SEASON

PREMIER DIVISION

Celtic	36	21	6	9	61	37	48
Rangers	36	18	9	9	52	35	45
Dundee United	36	18	8	10	56	37	44
Aberdeen	**36**	**13**	**14**	**9**	**59**	**36**	**40**
Hibernian	36	12	13	11	44	48	37
St. Mirren	36	15	6	15	45	41	36
Morton	36	12	12	12	52	53	36
Partick Thistle	36	13	8	15	42	39	34
Heart of Midlothian	36	8	7	21	49	71	23
Motherwell	36	5	7	24	33	86	17

1979-80 SEASON

PREMIER DIVISION

Aberdeen	**36**	**19**	**10**	**7**	**68**	**36**	**48**
Celtic	36	18	11	7	61	38	47
St. Mirren	36	15	12	9	56	49	42
Dundee United	36	12	13	11	43	30	37
Rangers	36	15	7	14	50	46	37
Morton	36	14	8	14	51	46	36
Partick Thistle	36	11	14	11	43	47	36
Kilmarnock	36	11	11	14	36	52	33
Dundee	36	10	6	20	47	73	26
Hibernian	36	6	6	24	29	67	18

1980-81 SEASON

PREMIER DIVISION

Celtic	36	26	4	6	84	37	56
Aberdeen	**36**	**19**	**11**	**6**	**61**	**26**	**49**
Rangers	36	16	12	8	60	32	44
St. Mirren	36	18	8	10	56	47	44
Dundee United	36	17	9	10	66	42	43
Partick Thistle	36	10	10	16	32	48	30
Airdrieonians	36	10	9	17	36	55	29
Morton	36	10	8	18	36	58	28
Kilmarnock	36	5	9	22	23	65	19
Heart of Midlothian	36	6	6	24	27	71	18

1981-82 SEASON

PREMIER DIVISION

Celtic	36	24	7	5	79	33	55
Aberdeen	**36**	**23**	**7**	**6**	**71**	**29**	**53**
Rangers	36	16	11	9	57	45	43
Dundee United	36	15	10	11	61	38	40
St. Mirren	36	14	9	13	49	52	37
Hibernian	36	11	14	11	48	40	36
Morton	36	9	12	15	31	54	30
Dundee	36	11	4	21	46	72	26
Partick Thistle	36	6	10	20	35	59	22
Airdrieonians	36	5	8	23	31	76	18

1982-83 SEASON

PREMIER DIVISION

Dundee United	36	24	8	4	90	35	56
Celtic	36	25	5	6	90	36	55
Aberdeen	**36**	**25**	**5**	**6**	**76**	**24**	**55**
Rangers	36	13	12	11	52	41	38
St. Mirren	36	11	12	13	47	51	34
Dundee	36	9	11	16	42	53	29
Hibernian	36	11	7	18	35	51	29
Motherwell	36	11	5	20	39	73	27
Morton	36	6	8	22	30	74	20
Kilmarnock	36	3	11	22	28	91	17

1983-84 SEASON

PREMIER DIVISION

Aberdeen	**36**	**25**	**7**	**4**	**78**	**21**	**57**
Celtic	36	21	8	7	80	41	50
Dundee United	36	18	11	7	67	39	47
Rangers	36	15	12	9	53	41	42
Heart of Midlothian	36	10	16	10	38	47	36
St. Mirren	36	9	14	13	55	59	32
Hibernian	36	12	7	17	45	55	31
Dundee	36	11	5	20	50	74	27
St. Johnstone	36	10	3	23	36	81	23
Motherwell	36	4	7	25	31	75	15

1984-85 SEASON

PREMIER DIVISION

Aberdeen	**36**	**27**	**5**	**4**	**89**	**26**	**59**
Celtic	36	22	8	6	77	30	52
Dundee United	36	20	7	9	67	33	47
Rangers	36	13	12	11	47	38	38
St. Mirren	36	17	4	15	51	56	38
Dundee	36	15	7	14	48	50	37
Heart of Midlothian	36	13	5	18	47	64	31
Hibernian	36	10	7	19	38	61	27
Dumbarton	36	6	7	23	29	64	19
Morton	36	5	2	29	29	100	12

1985-86 SEASON

PREMIER DIVISION

Celtic	36	20	10	6	67	38	50
Heart of Midlothian	36	20	10	6	59	33	50
Dundee United	36	18	11	7	59	31	47
Aberdeen	**36**	**16**	**12**	**8**	**62**	**31**	**44**
Rangers	36	13	9	14	53	45	35
Dundee	36	14	7	15	45	51	35
St. Mirren	36	13	5	18	42	63	31
Hibernian	36	11	6	19	49	63	28
Motherwell	36	7	6	23	33	66	20
Clydebank	36	6	8	22	29	77	20

1986-87 SEASON

PREMIER DIVISION

Rangers	44	31	7	6	85	23	69
Celtic	44	27	9	8	90	41	63
Dundee United	44	24	12	8	66	36	60
Aberdeen	**44**	**21**	**16**	**7**	**63**	**29**	**58**
Heart of Midlothian	44	21	14	9	64	43	56
Dundee	44	18	12	14	74	57	48
St. Mirren	44	12	12	20	36	51	36
Motherwell	44	11	12	21	43	64	34
Hibernian	44	10	13	21	44	70	33
Falkirk	44	8	10	26	31	70	26
Clydebank	44	6	12	26	35	93	24
Hamilton Acad.	44	6	9	29	39	93	21

1987-88 SEASON
PREMIER DIVISION

Team	P	W	D	L	F	A	Pts
Celtic	44	30	10	4	78	24	70
Heart of Midlothian	44	23	16	5	74	32	62
Rangers	44	26	8	10	85	34	60
Aberdeen	**44**	**20**	**17**	**7**	**55**	**26**	**57**
Dundee United	44	15	15	14	51	50	45
Dundee	44	18	7	19	71	63	43
Hibernian	44	12	19	13	41	43	43
Motherwell	44	13	10	21	37	56	36
St. Mirren	44	10	15	19	41	64	35
Falkirk	44	11	11	22	42	74	33
Dunfermline Athletic	44	9	10	25	45	81	28
Morton	44	3	10	31	27	100	16

1988-89 SEASON
PREMIER DIVISION

Team	P	W	D	L	F	A	Pts
Rangers	36	26	4	6	62	26	56
Aberdeen	**36**	**18**	**14**	**4**	**51**	**25**	**50**
Celtic	36	21	4	11	66	44	46
Dundee United	36	16	12	8	44	26	44
Hibernian	36	13	9	14	37	36	35
Heart of Midlothian	36	9	13	14	35	42	31
St. Mirren	36	11	7	18	39	55	29
Dundee	36	9	10	17	34	48	28
Motherwell	36	7	13	16	35	44	27
Hamilton Acad.	36	6	2	28	19	76	14

1989-90 SEASON
PREMIER DIVISION

Team	P	W	D	L	F	A	Pts
Rangers	36	20	11	5	48	19	51
Aberdeen	**36**	**17**	**10**	**9**	**56**	**33**	**44**
Heart of Midlothian	36	16	12	8	54	35	44
Dundee United	36	11	13	12	36	39	35
Celtic	36	10	14	12	37	37	34
Motherwell	36	11	12	13	43	47	34
Hibernian	36	12	10	14	34	41	34
Dunfermline Athletic	36	11	8	17	37	50	30
St. Mirren	36	10	10	16	28	48	30
Dundee	36	5	14	17	41	65	24

1990-91 SEASON
PREMIER DIVISION

Team	P	W	D	L	F	A	Pts
Rangers	36	24	7	5	62	23	55
Aberdeen	**36**	**22**	**9**	**5**	**62**	**27**	**53**
Celtic	36	17	7	12	52	38	41
Dundee United	36	17	7	12	41	29	41
Heart of Midlothian	36	14	7	15	48	55	35
Motherwell	36	12	9	15	51	50	33
St. Johnstone	36	11	9	16	41	54	31
Dunfermline Athletic	36	8	11	17	38	61	27
Hibernian	36	6	13	17	24	51	25
St. Mirren	36	5	9	22	28	59	19

1991-92 SEASON
PREMIER DIVISION

Team	P	W	D	L	F	A	Pts
Rangers	44	33	6	5	101	31	72
Heart of Midlothian	44	27	9	8	60	37	63
Celtic	44	26	10	8	88	42	62
Dundee United	44	19	13	12	66	50	51
Hibernian	44	16	17	11	53	45	49
Aberdeen	**44**	**17**	**14**	**13**	**55**	**42**	**48**
Airdrieonians	44	13	10	21	50	70	36
St. Johnstone	44	13	10	21	52	73	36
Falkirk	44	12	11	21	54	73	35
Motherwell	44	10	14	20	43	61	34
St. Mirren	44	6	12	26	33	73	24
Dunfermline Athletic	44	4	10	30	22	80	18

1992-93 SEASON
PREMIER DIVISION

Team	P	W	D	L	F	A	Pts
Rangers	44	33	7	4	97	35	73
Aberdeen	**44**	**27**	**10**	**7**	**87**	**36**	**64**
Celtic	44	24	12	8	68	41	60
Dundee United	44	19	9	16	56	49	47
Heart of Midlothian	44	15	14	15	46	51	44
St. Johnstone	44	10	19	15	51	66	39
Hibernian	44	12	13	19	54	64	37
Partick Thistle	44	12	12	20	50	71	36
Motherwell	44	12	12	20	46	61	36
Dundee	44	11	12	21	48	68	34
Falkirk	44	11	7	26	60	86	29
Airdrieonians	44	6	17	21	35	70	29

1993-94 SEASON
PREMIER DIVISION

Team	P	W	D	L	F	A	Pts
Rangers	44	22	14	8	74	41	58
Aberdeen	**44**	**17**	**21**	**6**	**58**	**36**	**55**
Motherwell	44	20	14	10	58	43	54
Celtic	44	15	20	9	51	38	50
Hibernian	44	16	15	13	53	48	47
Dundee United	44	11	20	13	47	48	42
Heart of Midlothian	44	11	20	13	37	43	42
Kilmarnock	44	12	16	16	36	45	40
Partick Thistle	44	12	16	16	46	57	40
St. Johnstone	44	10	20	14	35	47	40
Raith Rovers	44	6	19	19	46	76	31
Dundee	44	8	13	23	42	57	29

1994-95 SEASON
PREMIER DIVISION

Team	P	W	D	L	F	A	Pts
Rangers	36	20	9	7	60	35	69
Motherwell	36	14	12	10	50	50	54
Hibernian	36	12	17	7	49	37	53
Celtic	36	11	18	7	39	33	51
Falkirk	36	12	12	12	48	47	48
Heart of Midlothian	36	12	7	17	44	51	43
Kilmarnock	36	11	10	15	40	48	43
Partick Thistle	36	10	13	13	40	50	43
Aberdeen	**36**	**10**	**11**	**15**	**43**	**46**	**41**
Dundee United	36	9	9	18	40	56	36

1995-96 SEASON
PREMIER DIVISION

Team	P	W	D	L	F	A	Pts
Rangers	36	27	6	3	85	25	87
Celtic	36	24	11	1	74	25	83
Aberdeen	**36**	**16**	**7**	**13**	**52**	**45**	**55**
Heart of Midlothian	36	16	7	13	55	53	55
Hibernian	36	11	10	15	43	57	43
Raith Rovers	36	12	7	17	41	57	43
Kilmarnock	36	11	8	17	39	54	41
Motherwell	36	9	12	15	28	39	39
Partick Thistle	36	8	6	22	29	62	30
Falkirk	36	6	6	24	31	60	24

72